The
Writing
Game

50 evidence-informed writing activities for GCSE and A Level

Robin Hardman

First published 2021

by John Catt Educational Ltd,
15 Riduna Park, Station Road,
Melton, Woodbridge IP12 1QT

Tel: +44 (0) 1394 389850
Fax: +44 (0) 1394 386893
Email: enquiries@johncatt.com
Website: www.johncatt.com

ISBN: 978 1 913622 91 6

Set and designed by John Catt Educational Limited

REVIEWS

The Writing Game is a go-to guide for any teacher seeking to implement a succinct, evidence-informed approach to writing in the classroom. Where pedagogy around writing can sometimes veer towards the formulaic, resulting in mimetic rather than authentic outcomes for students, Robin Hardman provides a plethora of strategies with just the right amount of nuance and flexibility to ensure that teachers can make effective decisions about how to teach writing. I will be recommending this book to all teachers who wish to ensure their students are exposed to ways of responding to their subject in a way that is aligned with the best available evidence. An essential read.

Kat Howard

Head of professional learning at DRET Teaching School Hub and expert adviser at the Teacher Development Trust; author of Stop Talking About Wellbeing *and co-author of* Symbiosis: the curriculum and the classroom

If you're looking for a book full to the brim with practical classroom-based strategies then *The Writing Game* is for you. Robin Hardman takes you on a journey through a range of writing strategies linked to key pedagogy approaches. The activity outline, possible adaptations and top tips make each strategy accessible for teachers to consider how they can implement it into their own classroom. With direct reference to the research, *The Writing Game* will be a book you will lift on and off the bookshelf for many years to come.

Michael Chiles

Associate assistant principal at King's Leadership Academy Warrington; author of The Sweet Spot, The Feedback Pendulum *and* CRAFT

The Writing Game recognises the importance of the deliberate practice of extended writing and the isolated component skills that together make up skilled writing. Robin Hardman offers a range of practical examples from different subject areas that are flexible and adaptable. With the support of this book, teachers can help to remove the stigma around writing that prevents some students from achieving their best, as they view writing as an insurmountable barrier. Firmly rooted in research evidence of what works within the classroom, Hardman's tried-and-tested techniques can overcome this barrier and support students to achieve their full potential.

Kathrine Mortimore

Lead practitioner for English at Torquay Academy, Devon;
author of Disciplinary Literacy

The Writing Game is a great resource for teachers of all subjects. It is packed with practical, purposeful strategies to support students' writing across the breadth of the curriculum, helping them to crystallise and distil their knowledge and commit it to the page successfully. Robin Hardman acknowledges and explores the importance of deliberate writing practice in all subjects, and the strategies presented here are clear, adaptable and – vitally – rooted in pedagogy. From peer assessment and feedback to extended writing and redrafting, there is something for everyone in this handy book of bitesize tips for busy teachers, to help students' writing soar.

Amy Staniforth

Assistant principal at Iceni Academy Methwold, Norfolk;
co-author of Ready to Teach: Macbeth

For my parents

CONTENTS

Isolated skill practice

Extended writing

FOREWORD

Professional writers are not always able to put into words precisely what inspired a particular piece of writing. When they *are* able to do this, they offer explanations such as 'my writing was motivated by personal experiences', 'a careful study of gathered information', or 'a mental tussle with a thorny issue'. When they are less certain, their explanations become fuzzy and sometimes mystical, such as 'I follow my characters' lead' or 'It is like I am channelling my ideas from another source'.

Well, the inspiration for my preface for *The Writing Game* by Robin Hardman is quite certain. It was inspired by an earlier preface. In 1991, Karen Harris and I had dinner with the renowned American psychologist Donald Meichenbaum. At the time, we were finishing a book for teachers on how to help children become more strategic, knowledgeable and motivated writers. The instructional approach presented in this book, self-regulated strategy development, was stimulated by groundbreaking research conducted by Don. Before the dinner ended, we asked Don if he would write a preface for the book. He answered by telling us how he handled such requests: 'I keep a list of all the times I say no, so I will have time to do my own work.' Fearing all was lost, we were delighted when he gave us a playful smile and said: 'Of course I will do it.'

Over the years, the thing I remember most distinctly from Don's preface is that he quoted Kurt Vonnegut, the American novelist and satirist. I was a Vonnegut fan and I thought his quote was quite witty, if not demeaning to cosmetic consultants:

> *'... novelists ... have, on the average, about the same IQs as the cosmetic consultants at Bloomingdale's department store. Our power is patience. We have discovered that writing allows even a stupid person to seem halfway intelligent, if only that person will*

write the same thought over and over again, improving it just a little bit each time. It is a lot like inflating a blimp with a bicycle pump. Anybody can do it. All it takes is time.'

Writing is a wonderful thing. Its permanence makes it possible to ponder and reconsider the meaning and the value of the message. The basic message from Vonnegut is that writing can be improved. It just takes effort, revision and time. I agree with this message, but this observation assumes that the writer has the know-how and skills needed to make the message progressively better. This recommendation is best suited to competent and expert writers. Children are likely to find Vonnegut's advice frustrating. They are still in the process of acquiring the needed know-how and skills.

As I thought about Vonnegut's advice over the years, I frequently coupled it with another slice of sage wisdom also meant to be witty. Somerset Maugham, the famed novelist, proclaimed:

'There are three rules for writing a novel. Unfortunately, no one knows what they are.'

Maugham's satirical response about writing took aim at a common practice then and even today: self-declared experts providing the unwary with advice on how to be a successful writer. The antidote to this approach is to base recommendations about writing and learning to write on a more solid foundation.

During the last 100 years, we have learned a great deal about how writing operates and effective methods for teaching it. By reviewing thousands of research studies, my colleagues and I have identified basic principles for teaching writing. We know that children become better writers by writing. This is not enough, though, as they need to acquire basic writing know-how and skills. This includes strategies for planning, revising and editing; writing skills for converting ideas into acceptable sentences; spelling, handwriting and typing skills for converting these sentences into print; and knowledge about the basic purposes and methods of constructing different types of text.

We also know that we can help children produce their best writing by providing them with support as they compose. This includes setting clear goals for what their writing is to accomplish; engaging them in activities that help them collect, cull and organise possible writing content; and providing them with feedback. Writing is hard work and it is not always viewed by children or adults as enjoyable. Consequently, we need to use methods for teaching writing that are enjoyable and will help students become motivated writers. Finally, writing and reading draw on many of the same sources of knowledge and skills. We can facilitate writing as well as reading growth by using these two skills to support each other.

While no book on writing can provide you with everything you need to improve your students' or your child's writing, *The Writing Game* presents a variety of activities for improving children's writing. These activities engage students in meaningful writing tasks, teach students basic writing know-how and skills, and provide students with support as they write and learn. The activities address the most important principles acquired through the science of how to teach children to write:

Write

Teach

Support

The activities in *The Writing Game* address basic foundational skills in writing, including planning and revising, working with other writers, paragraph and sentence construction, and voice, to provide just a few examples. They also draw on proven instructional procedures such as modelling, scaffolding, guided practice, feedback and collaborative learning. Each activity includes suggestions for adapting the exercise to meet students' capabilities. Each activity is further based on one or more findings from the scientific literature. This is a unique feature not found in many books on teaching writing.

I hope you and your students (or child) enjoy *The Writing Game* as much as I did. I want to thank Robin Hardman for sharing these practices with us.

Steve Graham

Regents and Warner Professor, Arizona State University; Research Professor, Institute for Learning Sciences and Teacher Education, Australian Catholic University, Brisbane

INTRODUCTION

Writing well: it's a gift that some of us possess and others don't. It's not like we can do much to change that unfortunate educational fact, so why bother trying? Much better to focus on teaching subject content, surely, and hope that our lower-attaining students will be able to scribble down enough knowledge in an exam to scrape a half-decent mark. And as for the fortunate few who are blessed with an innate ability to write, well, they'll be absolutely fine, won't they? They already know how to write, so what's the point in hammering home skills that they've already mastered?

These attitudes might sound like common sense to many secondary teachers. They might be fairly close to the kinds of views you've heard uttered in the staff room or in department meetings. Maybe they're even positions that you've adopted yourself. The purpose of this book isn't to chastise or to stigmatise such points of view, and it's certainly not to reignite the age-old, zero-sum debate over the relative importance of knowledge and skills. (For what it's worth, both are clearly fundamental to a successful curriculum.) No, the reason why I'm highlighting these attitudes is that I used to let such perspectives go unchallenged, both in my own head and from my colleagues.

In a sense, my own upbringing had served to confirm those perceptions. I'm the son of two journalists and I was fortunate to grow up in a household that was full of books, newspapers and magazines. As a consequence, writing is one skill that I've never found particularly difficult. (Full disclosure: I find *lots* of other things incredibly challenging, from driving a car to figuring out how to open gates.) At school, essay subjects were a blissful refuge from the sheer terror of Maths problems and Chemistry practicals; at university, I was able to construct lines of argument that at least partially covered up my patchy attendance at lectures.

When I became a teacher after graduating, then, I assumed that children who hadn't grown up swallowing *The Times* before breakfast might always struggle to write to the standard that I desired. I didn't ignore writing skills in my first couple of years in the classroom. Far from it: I devoted substantial chunks of some lessons to telling my classes what I expected to see in their essays. I made checklists of the component parts of an A* paragraph; I wrote my own essays, photocopied them and expected my pupils to glory in their splendour. But seldom did I think about going beyond telling them *what* good writing entailed; even less frequently did I try to explain *how* they might improve.

For the best part of three years, I muddled on. The old A Level Politics course – my primary teaching responsibility – prioritised knowledge over analysis and evaluation, so the vast majority of my pupils were able to secure excellent grades without necessarily mastering the art of constructing an essay. But the new course, which I first started teaching in 2017, weighted each of those skills equally, and I soon became concerned about how many of my pupils struggled to explain the significance of their points and justify their lines of argument. When I asked fellow Politics teachers how they intended to close the gap between their pupils' written attainment and the demands of the new course, I was amazed at their laidback responses. It wasn't that they hadn't spotted the problems: they all recognised that their pupils were finding essay technique difficult to master. But nobody had a strategy for dealing with it.

I turned to teachers of other humanities and social science subjects, hopeful that they might offer some solutions. Although they all tried their best to help me, their responses contained few constructive suggestions. Most said things like, 'I just get my classes to write as many timed essays as possible.' Even the more helpful suggestions – like breaking essays down into discrete component skills, and following Black and Wiliam's 1998 recommendation of providing comments on pupils' work without the distraction of a mark – seemed only to offer partial solutions to a complex problem.

I'd always been interested in evidence-informed practice, so I started to root around for studies on writing development. To my great excitement, I discovered a wealth of research that could shape my instruction. The evidence base fell into three broad categories:

1. Some research confirmed assumptions that I'd already made, such as the fact that there's a correlation between the frequency of writing practice and the likelihood of pupils making progress.

2. Other studies were in line with well-known evidence about effective pedagogy and skill acquisition, such as the need for modelling, scaffolding and guided practice.

3. But I also discovered recommendations for effective instructional strategies that I'd never before considered, like group writing and redrafting exercises.

Taken together, these insights provide the basis for a robust, evidence-informed writing instruction program. And yet, although names like Barak Rosenshine, Daniel Willingham and Dylan Wiliam have rightly become part of everyday conversations among teachers, the work of researchers such as Steve Graham, Karen Harris and Gary Troia on writing instruction remains largely unknown in schools and colleges.

The Writing Game is the culmination of my efforts over the past three years to translate the insights of these researchers into my teaching practice. There are many barriers that prevent teachers from engaging with academic research, but recent years have seen the welcome rise of books (many of which have been published by John Catt) that aim to bridge the gap between research and classroom practice. My hope is that *The Writing Game* will contribute to this growing field by providing evidence-informed writing activities for busy teachers to use and reinterpret as they see fit.

Although *The Writing Game* can be read from cover to cover, you may prefer to treat it like a recipe book, using the contents list to help you find the activities that might work for your particular needs. An egg timer key indicates how much preparation is required for each activity: one egg timer means very little preparation is required, two egg timers mean some preparation will be necessary, and three egg timers indicate the need for a significant (though worthwhile) amount of preparation. Each activity contains at least one reference to the evidence base on effective writing skill instruction or effective pedagogy; a comprehensive list of references can be found at the back of the book.

This book aims to help busy teachers to understand and implement proven strategies for improving their pupils' writing skills. Although

I've aimed to make each activity engaging and enjoyable, nothing should distract from the core purpose of writing instruction, which is to aid writing development. The activities should be seen as facilitative means for achieving this goal, rather than as ends in themselves; they are unlikely to lead to substantial improvements in pupils' writing unless they are accompanied by expert instruction in the processes, skills and disciplinary literacy that form the constituent parts of effective writing in each academic subject.

Drawing on the work of Graham, Harris and Troia on writing instruction, and on research about effective teaching carried out by Rosenshine, Willingham, Wiliam and others, the activities that follow are based on seven overarching principles:

1. The more frequently pupils write, the greater the chance that they will make progress.
2. Teachers should guide writing practice for as long as possible, before gradually starting to remove the scaffolding.
3. Writing practice and knowledge recall can, and should, happen concurrently. The notion that teachers should prioritise either skills or knowledge is based on a false dichotomy.
4. As well as practising writing skills on an individual basis, pupils will benefit greatly from activities that require them to write in small groups.
5. Pupils should be in no doubt about what excellent writing entails in each of their subjects. Teacher modelling and peer assessment are therefore crucial components of effective writing instruction.
6. When providing pupils with commentary on their written work (whether addressed to individuals or to whole classes), teachers should abide by Wiliam's (2013) maxim that 'feedback should be more work for the recipient than the donor'.
7. Pupils should be required to undertake frequent self-reflection.

Of course, simply deploying some of these activities on an ad hoc basis will not be enough to maximise your pupils' chances of success. Writing skills should be woven throughout your teaching, so your pupils are frequently made aware of and reminded about the components of effective writing in your subject. It is crucial, too, that you do not try to fight a lone battle. Ideally, you should collaborate within and between departments to formulate common approaches to writing instruction. If you are a head of faculty or department, make sure your fellow teachers are, at the very least, dispensing common advice over essay technique; there are few things more confusing and demoralising for pupils than being given conflicting guidance by different teachers.

Regardless of your position, this is a call to arms to join the conversation about writing instruction over the coming weeks, months and years. The more brainpower that we collectively devote to improving writing skill instruction in schools and colleges, the greater the benefit to the young people in our care. It is incumbent on all of us, no matter our seniority or experience, to strive to elevate the status of writing instruction in our profession and our curricula.

Modelling

BASIC, BETTER, BEST

This *Antiques Roadshow*-inspired exercise makes a great starter or plenary activity. It can be used at any stage of a unit or topic, making it a versatile little number that quickly reactivates and tests pupils' understanding of the key writing skills that you're seeking to impart.

ACTIVITY OUTLINE

Provide your pupils with a handout containing examples of an introduction, a main paragraph or a conclusion from a short-answer or essay question of your choice.

In pairs or threes, pupils have to identify which example is the most basic, which is better and which is the best.

Once they have made their choices, ask them to discuss and jot down some brief bullet points explaining their decisions. Discuss as a class, addressing any misconceptions that arise and asking pupils why certain features are important.

What you'll need to prepare in advance

- Three examples each of an introduction, a main paragraph and a conclusion from a short-answer or essay question of your choice.
- A time-saving hack could be to use past pupils' work, although you'll need to take care to anonymise it.

Possible adaptations

1. If you want to fill a whole lesson, you could do this activity with entire essays rather than excerpts. Again, be careful about causing offence – use anonymised versions of past pupils' work.

2. If you have a little more time and don't mind committing grammatical murder, you could challenge your pupils to produce a 'bestest' version, acting on any areas for improvement that they can identify in the 'best' example.

3. You could turn this into a retrieval activity by using examples that answer questions from past topics.

Top tip

If you have time, follow this activity with a guided writing task such as Snakes and Ladders (page 82) or Para-Troopers (page 112).

Link to the evidence base

Rosenshine's (2012) finding that the most effective modelling must engage pupils' cognitive processing to require them to evaluate why an example constitutes effectiveness.

THE FISHBOWL

Warning: this isn't for the faint-hearted. The Fishbowl is an effective modelling and peer-assessment exercise to use with the right group of pupils, but if you're working with a really wide attainment range or if your pupils are particularly sensitive to criticism, it might not be the one for you. If this is the case, I'd recommend activities such as Essay Doctors (page 118), Draft Punk (page 134) or Para-Medics (page 138).

If you have a sufficiently robust group of pupils who are all capable of writing at a broadly similar standard, give The Fishbowl a whirl. You could either choose (as subtly as possible) your highest-attaining pupils, providing the rest of the set with a chance to learn from their approach, or you could select pupils lower down the attainment spectrum and task their peers with upskilling them.

ACTIVITY OUTLINE

Depending on the size of the class you're teaching, choose a certain number of pupils to enter into an imaginary fishbowl. (As a rule of thumb, I'd recommend aiming for a ratio of 1:4; so, if you have a class of 30, split your class into six groups of five. Each group would then have one pupil in their fishbowl and four pupils outside the fishbowl who can offer advice and constructive criticism.)

Using a shared document facility, a mini whiteboard or an old-fashioned piece of A3 paper, ask the pupils in the fishbowl to write an introduction/main paragraph/conclusion addressing a question that tests their knowledge of material you've recently covered.

> While they are writing, the pupils in their group outside the fishbowl should be offering suggestions, feedback and questions that probe their peers' understanding of why they're approaching the task in the way they've chosen. For example, 'Why have you decided to make that point first?' and 'Why is that sentence necessary?'

What you'll need to prepare in advance

Very little. If you're using shared documents, you might want to make them 'read-only' for the pupils not in the fishbowl, depending on whether you trust them not to sabotage their peers' work.

Possible adaptations

1. If you're looking to fill a whole lesson, you could do this activity with entire essays rather than individual paragraphs. Allocate different pupils to go into the fishbowl for the introduction, each paragraph and the conclusion.

2. Particularly if you're using this as a revision activity towards the end of a course, increase the level of challenge for the pupils in the fishbowl by limiting the observers to asking questions such as 'How could you explain that point further?' and 'What does that sentence need?' rather than making recommendations.

3. If you're feeling particularly brave, you could enter the fishbowl yourself, either on your own, in mock competition with one of your pupils, or with a departmental colleague. This might work well at an earlier stage of the course when you are trying to embed your pupils' understanding of key writing skills.

Top tip

Save the writing produced by those in the fishbowl for use in future activities like Basic, Better, Best (page 22) and Para-Medics (page 138).

Links to the evidence base

- Nestojko et al's (2014) finding that students who expect to have to impart knowledge and skills to others perform significantly better than those who don't.

- Kardas and O'Brien's (2018) finding that the more people watch someone else perform a skill, the more likely they are to believe they can perform the same skill themselves.

- Wiliam and Thompson's (2007) recommendation that teachers should activate pupils as learning resources for each other.

MARK MY WORDS

If you want to be a great teacher of writing, you have to be a great writer yourself. That doesn't mean you have to be some modern-day Proust or Joyce, but you do need to have a full understanding of what excellent writing entails in your subject, as well as the ability to produce models that can serve as exemplars for your pupils.

No matter how many fancy writing activities or pedagogical techniques we employ, the simple fact remains that our own expertise is the most valuable resource at our disposal, and knowing how and when to deploy it lies at the heart of effective teaching.

Mark My Words provides a focused and highly adaptable way of deploying your own expertise, allowing you to model excellence while also improving your pupils' ability to spot possible improvements.

ACTIVITY OUTLINE

Give your pupils a paragraph (or a full essay) addressing a question based on material that you've recently covered in class.

Using assessment criteria (either the exam board's or your own, if you feel the exam board's isn't written in accessible language), ask your pupils to mark your work, identifying its strengths and weaknesses.

Ask them to discuss in pairs or small groups initially and then lead a whole-class discussion, addressing any misconceptions that arise. If you have deliberately included a couple of knowledge or skill errors, ask pupils to come up with solutions in their groups.

What you'll need to prepare in advance

The paragraph or essay that you'd like your pupils to mark. You could use a previous pupil's work if you'd like to save time, but make sure you choose something that's sufficiently high quality. My recommendation would be to test your pupils' attention to detail by inserting a couple of deliberate knowledge or skill errors.

Possible adaptations

1. Combine Mark My Words with Argument Tennis (page 59), producing just half a paragraph and then asking your pupils to construct a counter-argument once they've marked your work.

2. If you have plenty of lesson time to fill, write only an introduction and a conclusion and ask your pupils to produce three main paragraphs (or however many you recommend in your subject) to follow the same line of argument.

Top tip

Test your pupils' understanding of what constitutes effective writing by asking questions such as 'Why is this sentence particularly effective?' and 'What makes that an A*/Grade 9 evaluation?'

Link to the evidence base

Troia's (2014) finding that learners are more likely to follow writing skill instruction delivered by teachers whom they perceive to be expert writers themselves.

Peer assessment

JUDGEMENT DAY

This is a handy series of activities that provide opportunities for generative recall, modelling, deliberate practice and peer assessment.

Judgement Day is designed to facilitate discussions about, and practice of, evaluation, a key skill at GCSE and A Level. I tend to use Judgement Day towards the end of a unit or topic, when my pupils have accrued enough knowledge about the subject content to begin to form their own opinions.

The tasks are configured to draw a distinction between balanced, justified judgements, which qualify for the Evaluation Nation, the heaven of the made-up religion Conclusionism, and one-sided, insufficiently explained judgements, which are consigned to Oversell Hell.

LESSON PLAN

1. Generative recall: Evaluative Epistles

You have been contacted by someone new to Conclusionism asking for your advice on how to make it into the Evaluation Nation (Conclusionism's heaven) and avoid being consigned to eternal misery in Oversell Hell.

In no more than three bullet points, what advice would you and your partner give them on how to write an effective conclusion? Add a further bullet point providing advice on how to avoid Oversell Hell.

2. Modelling: Scriptural Study

Read through the model conclusion on the board/lesson handout and discuss with your partner what makes it particularly effective. Which sentence constructions are used that facilitate balanced, justified judgements?

3. Deliberate practice: Judgement Day

Now it's your turn to attempt to make it into the Evaluation Nation. In your pairs, write your own conclusion to this question:

Henry VIII was a largely effective monarch from 1509-1529. Assess the validity of this view (25).

Make sure you heed the advice given by the Evaluative Epistles and the lessons gleaned from your Scriptural Study.

4. Peer assessment: Paragraph Purgatory

Swap your conclusion with another pair and decide whether theirs is sufficiently good to grant them entry into the Evaluation Nation, or if they should be consigned to Oversell Hell. As ever, make sure you explain and justify your judgement.

What you'll need to prepare in advance

- All you need to do in advance is to write or source a model conclusion on a question you have recently been considering with your class (but not the same question you want your pupils to consider).
- The model conclusion can be projected on a PowerPoint slide, or added to a lesson handout or topic booklet.

Possible adaptations

1. If you want to provide some scaffolding for pupils who struggle to form their own opinions about your subject, you could generate a series of possible lines of argument for them to choose from. For example:

    a. Henry VIII was far more effective in domestic policy than he was in foreign policy.

    b. Henry VIII was far more effective in foreign policy than he was in domestic policy.

    c. Despite some limited successes in both areas, Henry VIII was largely ineffective in domestic and foreign policy.

d. Despite some notable failures in both areas, Henry VIII was largely effective in domestic and foreign policy.

2. If you're pressed for time, you could move the peer assessment step to the next lesson, provide your own whole-class feedback at the beginning of the next lesson, or offer live feedback if you're using shared documents.

3. Alternatively, if you have a longer lesson to fill, you could add a fifth activity called The Second Coming, where pupils are able to improve their conclusions following feedback from the Paragraph Purgatory activity.

Top tips

- In your questioning, focus on interrogating your pupils' understanding of why certain language and sentence constructions enable particularly effective judgements.
- Challenge higher-attaining pupils by imposing constraints on the language they can use. For example, ask them to justify their judgement without using 'because', 'since' or 'as'.
- Refer back to the Evaluation Nation and Oversell Hell concepts in future feedback, modelling and deliberate practice activities. They can become part of your common language on writing skill instruction.

Links to the evidence base

- Troia's (2014) finding that group writing and modelling are important features of effective writing skill instruction.
- Wiliam's (2006) finding that learning happens best when pupils know what excellence looks like.
- Rosenshine's (2012) finding that the most effective teachers provide initial scaffolds for difficult tasks.

PARAGRAPH PURGATORY

Much like Sentence Saviours (page 130), Paragraph Purgatory is a useful plenary task that provides opportunities for retrieving prior knowledge of both subject content and writing skill objectives. Originally part of Judgement Day (page 30), this activity has developed into a quick, standalone way of drip-feeding some modelling into a content-heavy sequence of lessons.

ACTIVITY OUTLINE

Working in pairs or threes, pupils must consider the characteristics of an excellent paragraph. Briefly discuss as a whole class.

Using either a lesson handout or a projector, provide a series of paragraphs addressing essay or short-answer questions that you've recently covered in class.

In their small groups, pupils must decide whether each paragraph is good enough to qualify for Geography [replace with your own subject's name] Heaven, or if it suffers from such serious problems that it should instead be consigned to Geography Hell.

Discuss the merits and afflictions of each paragraph as a class.

What you'll need to prepare in advance

Taking care to anonymise the original authors, choose 3-5 paragraphs written by past pupils, perhaps as part of group writing tasks like The War of the Words (page 89) or Essay Triathlon (page 97). Make sure there's a nice mix of high, medium and low quality in order to activate your pupils' cognitive processing.

Possible adaptations

1. The activity can work just as well with introductions and conclusions as it does with main paragraphs. If you've used the Judgement Day activities in the past, you can revisit the concepts of the Evaluation Nation and Oversell Hell.

2. If you have a bit more time, you could induct your pupils into the Paragraph Priesthood, asking them to provide absolution for the weaker paragraphs by rewriting them without making any knowledge or skill errors. Provide sentence frames as a scaffold if necessary (see www.the-writing-game.com for examples that I've used in the past).

Top tip

Take some time to adapt the weaker paragraphs, inserting common knowledge and phrasing errors and then explaining why they constitute mistakes in your whole-class discussions.

Links to the evidence base

- Wiliam's (2006) emphasis on the importance of clarifying learning intentions and success criteria. Teachers should explain what excellence looks like.

- Troia's (2014) recommendation that teachers should provide activities in which students compare and contrast superior exemplars with inferior ones.

UPCYCLING

Similar to Levelling Up (page 110) and The Refinery (page 124), Upcycling is a highly adaptable starter or plenary activity that aims to develop pupils' understanding of how to produce high-quality writing.

Upcycling should be useful for learners across the attainment spectrum, but it's particularly aimed at those middle attainers who are struggling to make the improvements necessary for the jump into the highest grade brackets. Use it shortly before an assessment round as a way of encouraging more ambitious writing.

ACTIVITY OUTLINE

Using either a projector or a handout, provide your pupils with a basic but largely accurate paragraph relating to material that you've recently covered.

Working in pairs or small groups, pupils have to 'upcycle' the paragraph in accordance with your subject's mark scheme and the current attainment levels of your class. For instance, in a Politics lesson, I might ask my pupils to go through the following steps:

- Add more detailed examples.
- Introduce some explanations of significance linking back to the question.
- Produce a more detailed counter-argument.
- Fully justify why the chosen line of argument is most convincing.

Pupils must discuss their solutions as a as a group. You can model a worked example if necessary, or provide live feedback to each group.

What you'll need to prepare in advance

Just the paragraph you'd like your pupils to upcycle. As ever, it will save you plenty of time if you can use a previous pupil's (anonymised) work, adapting as you see fit.

Possible adaptations

1. Stretch your highest-attaining pupils by asking them to identify how the paragraph should be upcycled before beginning the task.

2. If you only have a very short period of time to spare, provide a paragraph with just one missing element (such as substantiated judgements or links back to the question) and task pupils with upcycling that particular feature.

3. If you have more time to fill, follow Upcycling with a peer-assessment task like Paragraph Purgatory (page 33) or Snakes and Ladders (page 82).

Top tip

Discuss why the changes you recommend are important to improving the paragraph, making reference to your subject's assessment objectives and your common language for writing development.

Link to the evidence base

Troia's (2014) recommendation that teachers should provide activities in which students compare and contrast superior exemplars with inferior ones.

Metacognition

ALIEN LANDING

If we were to compare writing skill instruction to cooking, Alien Landing would be like beans on toast or a Pot Noodle: quick and totally fuss-free, but undeniably satisfying. Although Alien Landing would work well in conjunction with any of the other activities in this book, I tend to use it just before an end-of-unit assessment, as a way of jogging my pupils' memory of what constitutes effective writing.

ACTIVITY OUTLINE

Depending on the disposition of your class, choose either a wildly enthusiastic or a deeply sarcastic tone to inform them that a spaceship has just landed in the playground/on the school roof/on the playing field. Keen to immerse themselves in their new planet's culture, the alien visitors would like to find out how to succeed academically.

In no more than five bullet points, your pupils must summarise the key ingredients of a successful essay in your subject. Discuss as a class, recording the best answers on the board so your pupils can refer to them once they start writing.

What you'll need to prepare in advance

This activity is oven-ready, with no preparation needed.

Possible adaptation

If you'd like to boost your pupils' metacognition further, you could follow Alien Landing with a quick round of Target Zone (page 40), allowing them to generate personal targets for the essay ahead.

Top tip

Make sure the summary bullet points you put on the board contain some of the language used in previous writing skill activities – for example, Judgement Jenga (page 52) and Oversell Hell (page 30).

Link to the evidence base

Willingham's (2006) finding that the best learning happens when pupils are required to think about something that activates their prior knowledge.

TARGET ZONE

A successful programme of writing instruction should satisfy two essential criteria. Firstly, learners should frequently be made aware of what excellent writing entails and given opportunities to practise strategies designed to make this high standard more accessible. Secondly, they should be in no doubt about what they need to do to close the gap between their own work and the exemplars they are shown. Hopefully, either or both of these aims are addressed in all the activities in this book, but rarely as explicitly as in Target Zone.

This is hardly the most imaginative activity contained in these pages, but it's a very effective way of narrowing your pupils' focus as they aim to make improvements to their writing. In the past, I've often used Target Zone in the run-up to mock or end-of-year exams, but it's an activity you should return to as frequently as possible.

ACTIVITY OUTLINE

Using recent essay feedback as a guide, ask your pupils to come up with a list of targets for each of the assessment criteria in your subject. It's best to focus on one particular style of question at a time.

Base your feedback for their next essay on whether they have met each of their targets.

What you'll need to prepare in advance

Absolutely nothing. Just ask your pupils to bring their recent essays with them to the lesson.

Possible adaptation

Rather than using this on an individual basis, you could use Target Zone before a group writing activity and then base your feedback to each group on whether they have met their targets.

Top tip

Encourage your pupils to update their targets frequently. After each essay would seem most appropriate, but they could also refine their targets after group writing exercises like Snakes and Ladders (page 82), The War of the Words (page 89) and Essay Triathlon (page 97).

Link to the evidence base

Troia's (2014) finding that effective writing instruction entails frequent opportunities for self-reflection and target-setting.

TOP TRUMPS

As with Target Zone (page 40), the purpose of this activity is to improve pupils' awareness of their own strengths and weaknesses as essay writers in your subject. If complemented by focused feedback and plenty of opportunities for deliberate practice, this should help to drive them towards reaching their potential.

ACTIVITY OUTLINE

Using recent essay feedback as a guide, ask your pupils to come up with a Top Trumps card for themselves as essay writers. A template is available at www.the-writing-game.com, but you can adapt the scoring system according to the particular demands of your subject.

For Politics, my scoring system would be as follows:

- Introduction-writing skills /100
- Ability to deploy detailed, accurate examples /100
- Ability to analyse and explain the significance of points /100
- Ability to form justified judgements /100
- Conclusion-writing skills /100

If you were a Modern Languages teacher, for example, you might wish to adapt the scoring system to the following:

- Language accuracy /100
- Ability to use different tenses /100
- Ability to deploy idioms /100
- Ability to make accurate cultural, social and historical references /100

> - Ability to analyse set texts/films with appropriate terminology /100
> - Ability to construct logical arguments /100
> - Ability to draw convincing conclusions /100

What you'll need to prepare in advance

Just the scoring system that you'd like your pupils to use for their own Top Trumps card. You might also wish to produce a rubric explaining what level of recent attainment would be necessary for scoring between 50 and 60, between 60 and 70, and so on. You can use your subject's marking grids to help you with this.

Possible adaptation

Depending on your cohort, you could adapt the theme of the activity to fit with their interests. For instance, I might ask a class of sport-obsessed pupils to create a FIFA profile for themselves, rather than a Top Trumps card. Or, even better, you could offer a choice of multiple mediums.

Top tip

Make their Top Trumps cards a live document updated after each essay. This is a great way of signposting your pupils' progress as the course evolves.

Link to the evidence base

Troia's (2014) finding that effective writing instruction entails frequent opportunities for self-reflection and target-setting.

DICTIONARY CORNER

Without wishing to become embroiled in the seemingly interminable debate over the relative importance of knowledge and skills in an academic curriculum, it's an unavoidable fact that possessing requisite subject knowledge is a pre-condition for effective writing. Indeed, without a firm grasp of the fundamental content, pupils will find almost all the activities in this book incredibly challenging.

Clearly, what you do in the rest of your teaching will have a huge impact on the quality of your pupils' understanding, but Dictionary Corner is one very simple way of trying to blend core knowledge retrieval with writing skill development.

ACTIVITY OUTLINE

Provide a list of core concepts relating to subject material that you have recently covered. Working in pairs or threes, pupils must write a definition for each concept.

Discuss the definitions as a class, addressing any misconceptions that arise.

What you'll need to prepare in advance

Just the list of core concepts, unless you opt for the second adaptation suggested below.

Possible adaptations

1. Give this activity a retrieval element by including a couple of concepts from earlier topics.

2. If you'd like to increase the level of difficulty, challenge your pupils to come up with a list of core concepts as the first stage of the activity. Discuss their lists as a class and then add anything that's missing. (This has the further benefit of removing any need for preparation on your part!)

3. You could combine this activity with Chains of Significance (page 63), asking your pupils to write sentences explaining the significance of each of these concepts once you've discussed the definitions.

Top tip

Encourage your pupils to keep a glossary of key terms and core concepts, which they should update frequently as the course progresses.

Link to the evidence base

Duin and Graves' (1987) finding that effective writing instruction involves a focus on 'definitional knowledge'.

LINGO BINGO

Worried that asking your pupils to write yet another paragraph will be met with cynical, ashen faces? There are plenty of activities in this book that might help you to jazz up writing practice, but Lingo Bingo explicitly plays on the sense of 'we've done all this a million times before' that tends to overcome pupils towards the end of a GCSE or A Level course.

It might work well at an earlier stage with a particularly high-attaining group, but my recommendation would be to use Lingo Bingo as a revision activity. It's a great exercise for testing pupils' content knowledge, writing skills and understanding of target language.

ACTIVITY OUTLINE

Working either as individuals or in small groups, pupils write a paragraph addressing a question you've been considering in your revision lessons.

As they do so, write down a list of target language (with appropriate synonyms) that you'd like them to use. For example:

- persuasive/convincing/plausible/accurate
- significant/noteworthy/indicative
- undermined/rebutted/overpowered by
- strengthened/supported/buttressed by
- exemplified/demonstrated/illustrated
- suggests/implies/denotes

Once they've finished writing, reveal your list. Any groups that have ticked off every item should shout 'Bingo!', with the first to do so awarded a prize.

What you'll need to prepare in advance

Absolutely nothing, if you're happy to generate the list of target language while your pupils are writing their paragraphs. If you'd like to provide live feedback instead (see the possible adaptation below), you can come up with your list in advance, which shouldn't take long.

Possible adaptation

As mentioned above, you could provide live feedback during the writing process, either by making use of a shared document facility, using mini-whiteboards or, in a time-honoured way, peering over your pupils' shoulders.

Top tip

Once the activity is over, make sure you spend some time checking your pupils' understanding of *why* each of the words or phrases on their bingo card are important components of essay technique, with reference to assessment objectives.

Link to the evidence base

Willingham's (2006) finding that the best learning happens when pupils are required to think about something that activates their prior knowledge.

Isolated skill practice

EVALUMATES

A short, quick-fire starter or plenary activity, Evalumates provides learners with an invaluable chance to practise evaluation, typically the most challenging skill in a humanities or social science discipline.

ACTIVITY OUTLINE

Using either a presentation or a handout, provide a stimulus statement relating to content you've recently covered. For example:

The US Supreme Court consists of politicians in robes.

Divide the class into pairs and ask each pair to number themselves 1 and 2. Ask the 1s to write a sentence agreeing with the statement and the 2s to write a sentence disagreeing with the statement. Next, ask them to discuss with their partner which line of argument they find more convincing, then produce an evaluative sentence justifying that opinion.

Repeat for as many statements as you see fit.

What you'll need to prepare in advance

I suggest preparing 3-5 stimulus statements, depending on how long you'd like the activity to take.

Possible adaptations

1. You could test your pupils' generative recall by including at least one stimulus statement relating to a topic covered earlier in the course.

2. If you're using this activity at the end of a topic, or as part of a revision programme, you could provide a list of essay questions rather than stimulus statements, and ask your pupils to write conclusions together for each one. If you have time, this could be followed by a peer-assessment exercise in which pupils provide feedback on each other's conclusions.

3. Challenge your highest-attaining pupils by imposing constraints on the language they can use to form their evaluations, prohibiting the use of common sentence constructions and vocabulary.

Top tip

If you've used the Judgement Day activity (page 30) in the past, refer back to the concepts of the Evaluation Nation and Oversell Hell, to aid pupils' memory of what constitutes an effective evaluation.

Link to the evidence base

Wiliam and Thompson's (2007) recommendation that teachers should activate pupils as learning resources for each other.

JUDGEMENT JENGA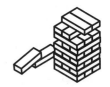

A couple of years ago, I noticed that too many of my pupils were sitting on the fence in their conclusions and end-of-paragraph judgements, meaning that their otherwise well-argued and detailed answers failed to reach the top level of the mark scheme.

My solution was to provide them with some sentence frames to use in their judgements, such as 'It is more convincing to argue that…' and 'Therefore, there is a more compelling case to be made for arguing that…'.

Although this tactic succeeded in steering most pupils away from weak conclusions, it also led to a classic case of unintended consequences. Having previously struggled to commit to a clear line of argument, my pupils suddenly started reaching excessively strident judgements that totally disregarded the merits of other perspectives.

Enter Judgement Jenga. Inspired by the beloved game, this activity helps pupils to produce evaluations that pick holes in weaker lines of argument without completely destroying them in a forced 'straw man' fashion.

ACTIVITY OUTLINE

Using either a handout or a projector, provide a series of one-sided arguments relating to material that you've covered recently. For example:

Henry VIII succeeded in pacifying potentially troublesome noble factions through his judicious use of patronage.

Explain the Jenga analogy, aided by an example of an excessively strident evaluation:

Henry VIII's heavy-handed treatment of Yorkist families like the Poles and the Brandons therefore proves that patronage was not an effective means of preventing possible challenges to his authority.

Working in pairs or threes, pupils need to consider how they might produce an evaluation that acknowledges the validity of the first argument while asserting the superior merits of the second.

As a class, model a solution. For example:

While Henry VIII did enjoy some success in pacifying the nobility through his use of patronage, his heavy-handed treatment of Yorkist families like the Poles and the Brandons shows that patronage was not the most effective means of preventing possible challenges to his authority.

Now ask each group to do the same for the rest of the statements on the handout/board. Discuss their solutions as a class.

What you'll need to prepare in advance

The one-sided statements and a model evaluation for one of them.

Possible adaptations

1. If you have time, and you'd like to increase the amount of generative recall involved, you could ask your pupils to produce the one-sided statements themselves. This has the added benefit of removing any need for advance preparation.

2. You could incorporate some knowledge retrieval by including at least one statement relating to content studied earlier in the topic, or in a previous unit.

3. If you'd like to fill a whole lesson, you could extend the activity by asking your pupils to write an entire paragraph, giving them a chance to practise the skills of building up a plausible weaker argument before asserting the merits of a stronger line of argument.

Top tip

Incorporate the Jenga analogy into your everyday practice and feedback – in my experience, pupils find it a useful reference point.

Link to the evidence base

Rosenshine's (2012) finding that the most effective teachers provide initial scaffolds for difficult tasks.

THE VICAR OF GLIBLY

If you find yourself frequently scribbling comments like 'More detail needed here' and 'Explain this point further' on your pupils' essays, The Vicar of Glibly is the perfect activity to encourage them to develop their responses. Equally suitable as a starter or a plenary, it should challenge pupils across the attainment spectrum.

ACTIVITY OUTLINE

Provide a handout/slideshow containing several vague or insufficiently substantiated statements relating to material that you've covered in the past. Ask your pupils to consider why these statements would benefit from more detail, perhaps steering their answers towards assessment objectives if appropriate.

Model a solution to one of the statements, writing or projecting a more detailed version on the board. Work through another model together as a class.

Give pupils the chance to work through 3-5 further statements in pairs or small groups, adding more detail to each one, and then provide whole-class feedback.

What you'll need to prepare in advance

A series of 5-7 vague or poorly explained statements and a solution to at least one of them.

Possible adaptations

1. If you have a little more time, you could ask pupils to produce their own statements and then share with another pair or small group.
1. If you're looking to fill a whole lesson, you could adapt this activity to use longer excerpts rather than standalone statements.
2. You could make this into a retrieval activity by using statements that relate to past topics.

Top tip

When demonstrating your model solution, highlight examples of sentence constructions that enable further elaboration. For example: 'This is significant because…', 'A further implication of this is that…', 'This exemplifies…', etc.

Link to the evidence base

Rosenshine's (2012) emphasis on the importance of explicitly addressing common misconceptions or recurrent issues with pupils' work.

MARY, MARY, QUITE CONTRARY

Similar to Judgement Jenga (page 52), Argument Tennis (page 59) and Counter Attack (page 75), Mary, Mary, Quite Contrary is a quick-fire starter or plenary activity that allows pupils to practise forming counter-arguments, a hugely important skill applicable across every humanities and social science discipline.

ACTIVITY OUTLINE

Project or write down a controversial statement relating to a topic area that you've recently covered. As a class, discuss why it might not be fully representative or accurate, and together work through an example of how it might be countered in an essay or shorter answer.

Then project or write down 3-5 additional statements that also relate to recent material. Working in small groups or as individuals, pupils have to produce counter-arguments for each statement.

Discuss their efforts as a whole class, asking pupils to peer-assess each other by judging whether the counter-arguments produced are as effective as they might be.

What you'll need to prepare in advance

Not very much, you'll be pleased to hear. If you're feeling uber-confident, you could come up with the statements off the cuff, but it might be safer to prepare a slide in advance.

Possible adaptations

1. You could introduce a peer-marking exercise afterwards. Ask pupils to assess whether each counter-argument produced by the other groups or individuals can be deemed effective and worthy of the category of 'Mary, Mary, Quite Contrary', or if they are excessively stark in how they expose the flaws in the original statement and should therefore be judged as 'Mary, Mary, *Too* Contrary'.

2. If you'd like to fill a longer period of time, write a one-sided paragraph containing a series of contestable lines of argument. Ask pupils to produce an extended counter-argument demonstrating its flaws.

3. Build in a retrieval element by including at least one statement that relates to material covered earlier in the course.

Top tip

Try this activity some time after using the Judgement Jenga activity (page 52). Remind pupils of the Jenga metaphor that explains the features of an effective counter-argument: expose the flaws in the original statement without attempting to trash its validity.

Link to the evidence base

Troia's (2014) finding that effective writing instruction requires a focus on writing effective sentences, before moving on to longer, more complex forms.

ARGUMENT TENNIS

Adaptable, focused and great fun, Argument Tennis is one of my favourite activities for building pupils' ability to analyse and develop their points.

Constructing two-sided arguments is essential in almost every humanities and social science discipline, yet too often we confine argumentation to debates and class discussions, rather than guiding pupils towards how to form and debunk written lines of argument. Equally suitable as a starter or a plenary (or even as a whole-lesson activity), Argument Tennis will add an invaluable string to your pedagogical racquet.

ACTIVITY OUTLINE

Working in pairs or threes, your pupils must produce a list of arguments relating to material that you've recently studied. Discuss as a class, then assign each pair or three another group to play Argument Tennis against.

Introduce the scoring system (adapt as appropriate for your subject): if there are any inaccuracies, unsubstantiated points or a lack of focus on the question, the team responsible automatically lose the rally; if only one team provide a detailed example then they automatically win the point.

Using either mini-whiteboards, a shared document facility or A3 paper, ask each group to write an extended rally explaining and defending one of the arguments or counter-arguments that you discussed as a class. For example, while one group write about how

> Henry VIII successfully used his powers of patronage, their opponents write about how his use of patronage was unsuccessful.
>
> Judge which group has won each rally, and repeat as many times as you like for different arguments/counter-arguments.

What you'll need to prepare in advance

Absolutely nothing, so long as you follow the first step in the activity outline. If you're pressed for lesson time, you could prepare a series of prompts in advance.

Possible adaptations

1. Vary the court surface for each rally, requiring pupils to move between quick-fire grass-court rallies with just one argument, supported by an example and an explanation, and longer clay-court rallies, where they have to build up a line of argument with multiple points, examples and explanations.

2. Make this into a whole-lesson activity by asking each group to write three half-paragraphs arguing against their opponents, judging the winner of the 'set' after each paragraph.

Top tip

Provide either a model or sentence frames to help your less confident pupils develop and defend their lines of argument.

Link to the evidence base

Graham's (2018) recommendation that teachers should create 'classroom writing communities'.

YOU'VE BEEN FRAMED

Two of the clearest indications provided by the evidence base on writing instruction are that scaffolding and guided practice are both crucial building blocks in developing long-term proficiency. Ideally suited for an early stage in pupils' writing development, although still a useful activity for later in a course of study, You've Been Framed provides both a scaffold and an opportunity for guided writing practice.

ACTIVITY OUTLINE

Provide your pupils with a series of sentence frames to help them write an introduction, a main paragraph or a conclusion. Working individually or in small groups, pupils need to use the sentence frames to complete the writing task that you've assigned.

Provide whole-class feedback, either while they are writing (if you have access to shared documents) or in the next lesson once you've had a chance to read what they have produced.

What you'll need to prepare in advance

The sentence frames you'd like your pupils to use. I recommend having a bank of these to suit different question styles and attainment ranges; the more frequently your pupils are exposed to them and encouraged to use them, the more likely they are to become embedded in their long-term memories.

Possible adaptations

1. Add peer assessment by combining this activity with an exercise like Paragraph Purgatory (page 33), Snakes and Ladders (page 82) or The Subs' Desk (page 126).

2. Introduce some differentiation by subtly providing groups/ individual pupils with different sentence frames depending on their recent levels of attainment.

3. If you're confident that your pupils have developed a reasonable understanding of how to construct effective introductions, conclusions or main paragraphs, challenge them to generate sentence frames for each other, making sure you vet the frames and address any problems that arise.

Top tip

Explain *why* the sentence frames you've provided help to produce effective writing, referencing specific assessment objectives if necessary.

Link to the evidence base

Rosenshine's (2012) finding that the most effective teachers provide initial scaffolds for difficult tasks.

CHAINS OF SIGNIFICANCE

Like The Vicar of Glibly (page 55), Chains of Significance is designed to improve pupils' understanding of how to develop their points. This time, though, there's a specific focus on encouraging detailed, rigorous analysis.

Although it could work as essay preparation, I tend to use this activity in the middle of a topic, once my pupils have started to build up enough knowledge to enable them to form meaningful connections and explanations.

ACTIVITY OUTLINE

Via a handout or a presentation, provide a stimulus statement such as:

Tony Blair's government suffered its first Commons defeat in 2005.

Divide the class into pairs or threes and ask them to discuss why that statement is significant. Then, as a class, model two or three sentences explaining the statement's significance, writing a coherent version of the answers on the board.

Working in small groups again, pupils must create chains of significance for the rest of the stimulus statements provided. Discuss their solutions as a class, asking them to add points that they didn't generate themselves.

What you'll need to prepare in advance

- I'd suggest preparing 3-5 stimulus statements, depending on how long you'd like the activity to take.

- If you're not confident about producing a live model, you could prepare one in advance.

Possible adaptations

1. You could give this activity a retrieval element by including at least one stimulus statement relating to a topic covered earlier in the course.

2. If you have time, you could follow the activity with a peer-assessment exercise, asking pupils to give feedback to other groups.

3. If you'd like to challenge your pupils a little more, you could combine Chains of Significance with Sentence Snowballs (page 65) to make Significance Snowballs, where each group must add to chains begun by other groups.

Top tip

Provide sentence frames to support your less confident pupils.

Link to the evidence base

- Willingham's (2006) finding that the best learning happens when pupils are required to think about something that activates their prior knowledge.

- Saddler and Graham's (2005) finding that explicitly teaching sentence-combining skills improves learners' writing development.

SENTENCE SNOWBALLS

Snow days aren't a thing of the past with this low-effort, high-impact activity that improves pupils' writing at a sentence-level while also developing their understanding of what constitutes an effective paragraph. Sentence Snowballs is an excellent starter or plenary that can easily be adapted depending on how much time you have.

ACTIVITY OUTLINE

Introduce an essay or short-answer question relating to content that you've recently covered. Working in pairs or threes, pupils write the opening sentence of an introduction, a main paragraph or a conclusion, depending on your preference.

Once they've written one sentence, ask each group to pass their work on to the group next to them. They then have responsibility for adding to the snowball by producing a sentence to follow the one written by the previous group.

Repeat this process for as long as it takes to complete an introduction, a main paragraph or a conclusion.

What you'll need to prepare in advance

You'll love this: absolutely nothing. You might want to ask your pupils to prepare an essay or paragraph plan in advance, but the activity works equally well if they are required to recall prior learning on the spot.

Possible adaptations

1. If you're looking to fill a whole lesson, you could combine Sentence Snowballs with a peer-assessment exercise like Paragraph Purgatory (page 33), asking each group to mark the paragraph that they began writing.
2. If you're able to use shared documents, you can provide live feedback to each group while they are writing.
3. If you'd like to challenge your pupils a little more, you could make this an individual exercise, rather than a group one.

Top tip
Provide sentence frames to support your less confident pupils.

Link to the evidence base
Saddler and Graham's (2005) finding that explicitly teaching sentence-combining skills improves learners' writing development.

RAPID-FIRE SENTENCES

As outlined in the introduction, one of the key components of a successful writing skills curriculum is frequent, deliberate practice. This sounds great in theory, but when the pressures of teaching content, marking and providing feedback on assessments, and building opportunities for retrieval practice into the curriculum begin to bite, writing skills activities can very easily tumble down the list of priorities.

Rapid-Fire Sentences is a starter or plenary activity designed to solve this problem. It's a quick but impactful way of building deliberate practice into a busy sequence of lessons. It can be adapted to suit any stage of a scheme of work, but it's perhaps best used once your pupils have been introduced to different writing skills and had the opportunity to practise them.

ACTIVITY OUTLINE

On the board, put up a series of prompts for sentences you'd like your pupils to write. For example:

1. Write a sentence providing evidence of Othello's sense of insecurity.
2. Write a sentence comparing Othello and Mr Rochester's characterisation.
3. Write a sentence outlining a similarity between Desdemona and Jane Eyre.
4. Write a sentence judging how far Othello can be considered to be defined by his race.
5. Write a sentence judging how far *Othello* and *Jane Eyre* are tales of jealousy.

What you'll need to prepare in advance

Only 3-5 prompts. You could come up with these off the cuff, if you like, but my recommendation would be to prepare a handout or presentation in advance.

Possible adaptations

1. You could introduce a peer-marking exercise afterwards, or at the beginning of the next lesson, asking pupils to assess how effective their peers' sentences are.

2. If you'd like to fill a longer period of time, produce a series of prompts that build up to a whole paragraph.

3. Inject some retrieval practice into the activity, including at least one statement that relates to material covered during a previous topic.

Top tip

Provide sentence frames for your less confident pupils. Make sure you discuss what constitutes an effective example of each sentence type, asking questions like 'What makes an effective judgment?' and 'What kind of language can we use to facilitate comparisons across texts?'

Link to the evidence base

Troia's (2014) finding that effective writing instruction requires a focus on writing effective sentences, before moving on to longer, more complex forms.

SO, WHAT?

Like The Vicar of Glibly (page 55) and Chains of Significance (page 63), So, What? aims to improve pupils' ability to develop their points, which is often a differentiating factor between middle- and high-attainers.

A highly adaptable starter or plenary activity, So, What? can be used at any stage of a topic or a course, either as a retrieval exercise designed to activate pupils' memory of content studied some time ago, or as a way of testing their understanding of material covered in recent lessons.

ACTIVITY OUTLINE

Provide a list of factually accurate statements, examples or quotations (depending on your subject matter) on the board/screen.

Working in small groups, pupils must discuss why each statement is significant and then write an accompanying explanation using the sentence frames provided. Discuss their explanations as a class.

What you'll need to prepare in advance:

- I'd suggest preparing 3-5 stimulus statements, depending on how long you'd like the activity to take.
- Unless you'd like the activity to be particularly taxing (if you've almost finished the course or you have a very high-attaining set), you should also prepare some sentence frames to help your pupils develop their explanations.

Possible adaptations

1. In order to provide a balance between retrieval practice and assessment for learning, you could include a mix of statements relating to material that you've recently covered and others relating to previous topics.

2. If you have more time to fill, you could ask your pupils to write a series of sentences for each prompt, rather than just a single explanation, challenging them to think of other statements, examples or quotations that could be used to support the one you've provided.

3. If you'd like to increase the level of difficulty further, you could ask your pupils to come up with the statements themselves and then share with another group.

Top tip

Work through a model as a class, taking care to explain *why* explanations are so important, with reference to assessment objectives if appropriate.

Link to the evidence base

Troia's (2014) finding that effective writing instruction requires a focus on writing effective sentences, before moving on to longer, more complex forms.

THE HIGHWAYS AGENCY

How often do you find yourself scribbling (if you're anything like me, with increasingly aggressive pen strokes) exclamations like 'Answer the question!' and 'Link back to your line of argument!' on your pupils' essays? As a conservative estimate, I'd guess that comments of this kind account for nearly a quarter of the feedback that I write on my pupils' A Level Politics essays.

Equally useful as a starter or a plenary activity, The Highways Agency aims to reduce such exasperation (and, more importantly, to boost pupils' ability to actually address the question they are supposed to be answering) by providing deliberate practice of signposting. One of the best pieces of advice I received at school came from a History teacher who told me they should be able to work out the question being answered and the line of argument from reading only the first and last sentences of each paragraph in an essay. This is a mantra that I repeat ad nauseam to my own pupils.

ACTIVITY OUTLINE

Provide your pupils with a paragraph or essay shorn of links to the question. After checking their understanding of what constitutes an effective signpost sentence, ask them to read the paragraph provided and then, working either as individuals or in small groups, add signpost sentences at the beginning and the end of the paragraph. (Depending on your essay structure, you might want to ask them to produce a signpost in the middle of the paragraph, too.)

Discuss their solutions as a class and address any misconceptions that arise.

What you'll need to prepare in advance

Just the paragraph or essay that you'd like your pupils to add signposts to. Rather than going to the effort of writing one yourself, use a paragraph produced by a pupil/group of pupils in the past – perhaps in a group writing activity like The War of the Words (page 89) or Essay Triathlon (page 97) – and amend accordingly.

Possible adaptations

1. If you have more time to fill, you could combine The Highways Agency with a longer redrafting task like Essay Doctors (page 118), The Refinery (page 124) or Para-Medics (page 138).

2. Rather than providing your pupils with a paragraph or an essay, you could ask them to come up with their own signpost sentences for an essay they've recently planned, or one they'll be writing in the near future.

3. If you feel your pupils would be better served by practising the construction of whole paragraphs, rather than just signpost sentences, you could provide them with the signposts for a paragraph that they then have to write themselves. (This activity would be similar to You've Been Framed on page 61.)

Top tip

Embed these skills in the long term by requiring your pupils to produce signpost sentences every time they plan an essay.

Link to the evidence base

Troia's (2014) finding that providing instruction on paragraph structure is a hallmark of effective writing pedagogy.

TELL ME WHY

Even if you're not a fan of the Backstreet Boys (although why wouldn't you be?), this is a brilliant activity that you can use at every stage of a course or topic. Drawing on dual coding theory as well as the evidence base on writing skill instruction, Tell Me Why has the twin benefits of generating knowledge recall and providing deliberate, sentence-level practice.

ACTIVITY OUTLINE

Using either a presentation or a handout, provide your pupils with 3-5 pictures of people who are relevant to content you've recently covered. Depending on the subject you teach, they might be characters, theorists, critics or historical figures.

Working in pairs or small groups, pupils write a sentence or series of sentences explaining why the people in each picture are significant. If you like, you can give them an essay or a short-answer question to guide their writing.

Discuss their sentences as a class, addressing any misconceptions that emerge and working through models if necessary.

What you'll need to prepare in advance

Just the pictures that you'd like to use as prompts. Make sure your pupils have seen pictures of these people in the past, but try to strike a balance between pictures that are straightforward to write about and more challenging ones.

Possible adaptations

1. You could combine Tell Me Why with The Generation Game (page 106), challenging pupils to write a paragraph that mentions the people pictured.

2. Add some retrieval practice by including at least one picture that relates to an earlier topic.

3. If you have more time to fill, and if it suits the demands of your subject, you could use pictures of people who disagree with each other or can be used as examples to support different lines of argument, and then ask your pupils to construct a balanced, two-sided paragraph. For instance, if I were covering a question on the extent of the Prime Minister's power, I might have pictures of Tony Blair and Theresa May, encouraging my pupils to consider how executive power can ebb and flow according to circumstances. Or, if I were looking at a question on utilitarianism, I might use pictures of John Stuart Mill and Jeremy Bentham, prompting pupils to consider how they differ on the issue of higher and lower pleasures.

Top tip

Provide sentence frames to help your less confident pupils develop their explanations.

Link to the evidence base

Mayer and Anderson's (1991) findings in favour of dual coding's positive impact on long-term learning.

COUNTER ATTACK

Like its close relatives, Mary, Mary, Quite Contrary (page 57) and Argument Tennis (page 59), Counter Attack is a useful starter or plenary activity that hones pupils' ability to produce counter-arguments under time pressure.

ACTIVITY OUTLINE

Divide the class into small groups. Using a prompt relating to material you've recently covered (for example, the Henrician Reformation or the benefits of globalisation), ask each group to produce two sentences outlining a point that is supported by evidence.

Next, ask each group to swap their sentences with another group, who are now responsible for generating a counter-argument that is supported by evidence.

Repeat 2-4 times, depending on how long you would like the activity to last.

What you'll need to prepare in advance

Just the prompts.

Possible adaptations

1. If you'd like to fill a longer period of time, ask each group to produce a one-sided paragraph containing a series of contestable lines of argument. Once they've swapped with another group, they are then charged with writing the other half of the paragraph, demonstrating the flaws in the lines of argument produced by the first group.

2. Turn this into an oracy activity, rather than a writing skills one. Divide the class into pairs and ask each pair to number themselves 1 and 2. For the first prompt, ask the number 1s to put forward an argument and the number 2s to provide a counter, and then swap their roles for each subsequent prompt. You could also ask them to write up each other's arguments using the sentence frames provided.

3. You could combine this activity with Judgement Jenga (page 52), asking pupils to produce a balanced judgement that synthesises the most persuasive aspects of the arguments and counter-arguments that they produce.

Top tip

Provide some sentence frames to support your less confident pupils.

Link to the evidence base

Troia's (2014) finding that effective writing instruction requires a focus on writing effective sentences, before moving on to longer, more complex forms.

5-5-1

No, this isn't a groundbreaking football formation. 5-5-1 is a brilliant activity that can be used just as well for knowledge retrieval as for writing skill practice. If I use it for the former, this tends to be at an early stage of a topic, when I want to test pupils' understanding of content that they've recently encountered for the first time. In these instances, I ask them to write five bullet point sentences summarising what we studied in the previous lesson or sequence of lessons. Then they need to reduce those five sentences to five words and finally to one word.

If I use the activity primarily for writing skill practice (though it would still have a retrieval element), I ask my pupils to produce five sentences of varying types (see below for examples). In the second stage, they reduce these to a five-word judgement and finally to a one-word summary.

ACTIVITY OUTLINE

On the board, project a series of prompts for the five sentences that you'd like your pupils to write. For example:

1. Write a sentence providing evidence that the Weimar Constitution contained weaknesses.

2. Write a sentence arguing, with evidence, that the weaknesses in the Weimar Constitution were not the sole reason why the Nazis rose to power.

3. Write a sentence outlining why the Great Depression played a role in the Nazis' rise to power.

4. Write a sentence arguing that the Treaty of Versailles was a less important factor in the Nazis' rise to power than the Great Depression.

5. Write a sentence demonstrating your awareness of the interplay between the short- and long-term factors that led to the Nazis' rise to power.

Next, ask your pupils to reduce their sentences to a five-word judgement on why the Nazis rose to power. Finally, ask them to reduce that judgement to a single word.

Here's an example of how this might work in practice:

Write five sentences summarising how the Nazis developed their ideology

1. The Nazis took advantage of the Great Depression, promising to re-energise the German economy by providing employment through major public works programmes.

2. Hitler exploited a deep-seated sense of injustice among many Germans at the harsh terms of the Treaty of Versailles, pledging to remilitarise, unite all German-speaking peoples and create *Lebensraum.*

3. The Nazis disseminated anti-Semitic propaganda alleging that Jews were not true Germans and claiming they were to blame for both Germany's defeat in the First World War and the Great Depression.

4. They also fabricated pseudo-scientific studies suggesting that the 'Aryan race' was superior to all other races, and particularly to Jews.

5. Nazism was totally opposed to Communism, which was considered to be dangerously expansionist and a threat to German nationalism.

Reduce to five words

1. Employment.
2. *Lebensraum.*
3. Anti-Semitism.
4. Exceptionalism.
5. Anti-Communism.

> **Reduce to one word**
> 1. Propaganda.

What you'll need to prepare in advance

Only the five initial prompts. As ever, you could produce these on the spot, but the quality of the practice is likely to be better if you consider them in advance.

Possible adaptations

1. If you're pressed for time, you could cut the activity to 3-1-1, asking your pupils to produce just three initial sentences and then a one-sentence judgement, before reducing to one word.

2. If you've used the Judgement Day activity (page 30) in the past, you could ask pupils to assess whether each other's judgements would qualify for the Evaluation Nation or if they should be consigned instead to Oversell Hell.

3. You could design the five sentences so they build up an introduction, a conclusion or a mini-paragraph. You could either put them in the correct sequence or jumble them up (see Rumble in the Jumble on page 140) and ask pupils to decide which sequence would be best.

Top tip

Provide sentence frames for your less confident pupils. Remember to probe their understanding of what constitutes an effective example of each sentence type, asking questions like 'What makes a justified judgment?' and 'What kind of language can we use to demonstrate our understanding of causation?'

Link to the evidence base

Willingham's (2006) finding that the best learning happens when pupils are required to think about something that activates their prior knowledge.

Extended writing

SNAKES AND LADDERS

This spin on a children's classic is one of my favourite whole-lesson writing activities, providing a framework for deliberate practice that simultaneously stretches the highest attainers and supports those who find writing more difficult.

My recommendation would be to deploy it shortly before a formal assessment, giving your pupils a chance to challenge themselves and make mistakes in a low-stakes environment before they face the pressure of a timed essay.

It's also a fun, engaging way of revising, providing a break from the monotony of practice papers and knowledge quizzes.

LESSON PLAN

Divide the class into small groups (pairs or threes tend to work well). Using a slide or a handout, outline the criteria for moving along the board, and the criteria for the snakes and the ladders. For example:

- One square: a grammatically correct sentence.
- Two squares: an accurate example or plausible explanation.
- Three squares: a detailed example or explanation.
- Four squares: a justified judgement.
- Five squares: an explanation that links back to the question.
- Six squares: an effective counter-argument.
- Snakes: phrasing errors; unsubstantiated points; inaccurate examples; unjustified judgements.

> • Ladders: multi-skill sentences; using cross-topic examples; referring to critics' interpretations.
>
> Ask each group to write a paragraph answering a pre-planned essay question. Swap the paragraphs between groups, asking them to assess their classmates against the rubric above. Once a paragraph makes it to a snake or a ladder, it can only slide or climb if it has already satisfied one of the specified criteria.
>
> Ask the class if anyone thinks the paragraph they've marked has made it to the 100th square (the end of the board). If so, review as a class and decide whether you all agree that the paragraph is of sufficiently high quality. If not, review the highest-scoring paragraph and then ask each group to improve it so it makes it to the end of the board.

What you'll need to prepare in advance

- You'll need to find a Snakes and Ladders board online (you can download mine from www.the-writing-game.com) and then decide on the criteria you want to use.

- Remember to ask your pupils to produce a paragraph plan in advance. This will allow them to focus more on their writing skills during the activity, rather than having to spend time recalling knowledge.

Possible adaptations

1. If you're confident your pupils have a good understanding of what constitutes an effective paragraph, ask them to generate possible scoring criteria in their groups and then agree on a common rubric as a class.

2. Alternatively, you could keep your criteria hidden until after each group has finished writing, challenging your pupils to second-guess what you're looking for.

3. If your pupils are able to use shared documents, you can provide some live feedback to each group while they are writing. Rather than telling them exactly what they've got wrong, you could ask

questions like 'Why do you think you might be in danger of sliding down a snake in the opening sentence?' or 'How could you move five squares rather than three in the fourth sentence?'

Top tips

- Keep copies of each group's paragraphs for use in future modelling activities like Basic, Better, Best (page 22), Paragraph Purgatory (page 33) and The Subs' Desk (page 126).

- When discussing your scoring criteria, remember to probe pupils' understanding of why certain sentence constructions are particularly effective or ineffective, making reference to your subject's assessment objectives if appropriate.

- During the whole-class discussion on the highest-scoring paragraphs, discuss how the authors could have scored even more highly by making small tweaks to their phrasing, evidence, explanations or judgements.

Links to the evidence base

- Rosenshine's (2012) finding that the most effective modelling must engage pupils' cognitive processing, requiring them to evaluate why an example is effective, and Rosenshine's emphasis on the importance of explicitly addressing common misconceptions.

- Graham's (2018) finding that the most effective writing instructors create 'classroom writing communities' in which pupils frequently collaborate on low-stakes writing tasks.

- Wiliam's (2006) finding that peer and self-assessment are crucial to maximising pupils' progress.

THE GREAT BRITISH WRITE OFF

Teaching is rather like writing a recipe book. We can provide step-by-step instructions on how to write an introduction, a paragraph, a conclusion or an entire essay, and we can help our pupils to understand how they might use certain ingredients in different situations. But, ultimately, they are the chefs, charged with following the recipes we've crafted for them, adapting to unforeseen circumstances, and choosing which alternative ingredients to use if the supermarket shelves are bare.

The Great British Write Off riffs on this analogy, allowing you to offer as much guidance as you think necessary while providing pupils with a chance to engage in deliberate practice. The activity works equally well with pupils writing independently or in small groups, although I tend to prefer the latter: I think pupils can learn plenty from each other in discussions about phrasing, the execution of challenging skills like evaluation, and the deployment of accurate supporting evidence.

LESSON PLAN

Working in small groups, pupils must consider how they would respond to an essay or short-answer question that covers material you've recently taught. Once they've done this, hold a brief whole-class discussion about how they might approach the question, addressing any misconceptions that emerge from their answers.

Introduce them to the 'Technical Challenge' recipe that you've prepared, probing their understanding of why an effective introduction/paragraph/conclusion/whole answer requires these ingredients. In their groups, the pupils follow the recipe and award a prize for the best one. For example:

Evaluate the view that Parliament is no longer fulfilling its key functions effectively (30).

Parliamentary Pavlova

Ingredients:

- Three sentences signposting a clear, justified line of argument.
- Four detailed examples (two supporting each side of the argument).
- Four accompanying explanations of significance.
- One link to the Elections and Referendums topic.
- One sentence containing a 'While it is true that…, it is more often the case that…' construction.
- One 'although'.
- One 'untypical' or 'anomalous'.

Method:

- Signpost the stronger line of argument in your opening sentence.
- Acknowledge the merits of the weaker line of argument (with two supporting examples and explanations).
- Assert the superiority of the stronger line of argument (with two supporting examples and explanations).
- Justify your chosen line of argument and link back to the question.

What you'll need to prepare in advance

- Your recipe. Depending on the nature of your cohort and the stage you've reached in the course, this can either break down the task in exhaustive, step-by-step detail, or give a brief overview that requires pupils to activate their prior knowledge of writing skills.

- If you'd like to provide extra support for your less confident pupils, you could also prepare a larder of ingredients (sentence frames, relevant examples or lines of argument) for them to use.

Possible adaptations

1. If you have plenty of lesson time to fill, and particularly if you're using this as a revision activity at the end of a course, you could follow the 'Technical Challenge' with a 'Showstopper Challenge', asking pupils to write an outstanding introduction, paragraph or conclusion answering a question of their choice.

2. You could add another level of difficult by pausing the class roughly halfway through the activity and informing pupils that a shortage of ingredients means they have to complete the challenge without using common words like 'however', 'although' and 'while' – or, if you'd prefer, without using a particularly well-known example. This will force them to consider alternatives, which should improve their range of language/knowledge.

3. Add a peer-assessment element by asking pupils to channel their inner Mary Berry, Prue Leith or Paul Hollywood and provide feedback on the writing produced by their peers.

4. If you have lots of faith in your pupils, try casting them as chefs *and* recipe authors, asking them to write recipes for another pupil or group.

Top tips

- This may sound obvious, but make sure you really think about what you'd like your pupils to get out of the task while you plan your recipe. Design each part of the recipe with a deliberate focus on something they find particularly difficult, or on introducing a new skill that you'd like pupils to practise in low-stakes conditions.
- If you have access to shared documents, make use of it. Live feedback can be such a valuable tool for addressing small problems that you might not have time to discuss in whole-class feedback.

Links to the evidence base

- Rosenshine's (2012) finding that the most effective teachers provide initial scaffolds for difficult tasks.
- Wiliam's (2006) finding that peer and self-assessment are crucial to maximising pupils' progress.
- Graham's (2018) finding that collaborating in groups improves learners' writing skills.

THE WAR OF THE WORDS

Like Essay Jet (page 93) and Essay Triathlon (page 97), The War of the Words is a stimulating and engaging group writing activity that takes an entire lesson (see the 'Possible adaptations' section for a shorter version). It works equally well as a way of considering an essay question based on recently covered content, in place of a traditional end-of-unit essay, or as a revision activity.

LESSON PLAN

Starter: Battle Planning

In pairs, pupils must agree on three goals for the task ahead, one for each of the skills below:

- Knowledge and understanding.
- Analysis.
- Evaluation.

Main

Stage 1: Opening Exchanges. Ask each group to write an introduction to a pre-planned essay question. Provide the prompts below to remind them of the component skills you'd like them to practise:

- Show off your military capabilities with an early statement of strength (define key terms).
- Demonstrate your force's ability to fight in a versatile fashion (discuss a two-sided argument).

- Make an initial assault on the enemy (direct your answer to the question).

Stage 2: Murderous Middle. Ask each group to write a main paragraph, using the following prompts:

- Lure the enemy in by setting a trap (present the weaker side of the argument).
- Then destroy with a vicious counter-attack (assert the merits of the stronger side of the argument).
- Establish your authority by securing the ground you've gained (produce an evaluation that demonstrates why one side of the argument is more persuasive than the other).

While pupils are writing their paragraphs, mark the introductions (awarding five points for each of the bullet-point prompts) and write the scores on the board.

Stage 3: Final Flourish. Ask each group to write a conclusion, using the prompts below:

- Demonstrate your army's capability one last time (answer the question).
- Provide a reminder of your versatility (acknowledge the merits of the weaker side of the argument).
- Prove you are victorious (explain why your chosen side of the argument is more persuasive).

While pupils are writing their conclusions, mark their main paragraphs (awarding 10 marks for each of the bullet-point prompts) and add the scores to the totals from Stage 1. Mark the conclusions before the next lesson, when you can reveal the overall winner and undertake some peer assessment.

What you'll need to prepare in advance

- Along with Essay Triathlon and Essay Jet, The War of the Words requires little preparation. Ask pupils to prepare an essay plan for their homework, so that in class they can focus more on practising writing skills than on knowledge recall.

- Produce some accompanying slides with prompts for each of the three stages. If you'd like to save time, you can adapt my presentation (available at www.the-writing-game.com).

Possible adaptations

1. If you're pressed for time, or if you'd prefer to focus on practising technique for individual paragraphs rather than whole essays, you could change the stages to the following:

- **Opening Exchanges**: lure the enemy in by setting a trap, building up the weaker side of the argument.

- **Murderous Middle**: having lured the enemy in, now demonstrate the extent of your army's capabilities by asserting the merits of the stronger side of the argument, unpicking problems with the weaker side as you do so.

- **Final Flourish**: secure your victory with an end-of-paragraph evaluation explaining why your chosen line of argument is more persuasive.

2. If you have the technological capability for creating shared documents, you can provide live feedback to each group while they are writing.

3. If you don't mind inducing sniggering from your class, you can give yourself the role of Military Headquarters, encouraging pupils to make radio contact with you if they need help with a phrasing or knowledge question.

Top tips

- Think carefully about the groups that pupils are working in. Sometimes you might want to group by attainment level, but at other times it can be useful to have mixed attainment groups.
- Encourage every member of each group to take responsibility for being the scribe in at least one of the stages.
- Challenge higher-attaining pupils to use complex target vocabulary.
- Use excerpts from the work produced for peer assessment or modelling activities in the next lesson.

Links to the evidence base

- Graham's (2018) finding that the most effective writing instructors create 'classroom writing communities' in which pupils frequently collaborate on low-stakes writing tasks.
- Wiliam's (2013) recommendation that tasks should be designed to elicit evidence of learning and lead to responsive teaching that addresses imperfections.

ESSAY JET

Like The War of the Words (page 89) and Essay Triathlon (page 97), Essay Jet is a great whole-lesson activity that can be used either midway through a topic for exploring an essay question on recently covered material, later in a topic instead of a traditional end-of-unit essay, or as a revision activity.

LESSON PLAN

Starter: Route Mapping

In pairs, pupils must agree on three goals for the task ahead, one for each of the skills below:

- Knowledge and understanding.
- Analysis.
- Evaluation.

Main

Stage 1: Take-Off. Ask each group to write an introduction to a pre-planned essay. Provide the prompts below to remind them of the component skills you'd like them to practise:

- Welcome passengers on board and reassure them by establishing your credentials and expertise (define key terms).
- Complete all necessary checks of the cockpit and cabin (discuss two-sided argument).
- Build up sufficient speed on the runway to take off smoothly (direct your answer to the question).

Stage 2: Flight. Ask each group to write a main paragraph, using the following prompts:

- Reassure passengers that take-off went smoothly (signpost strong argument in one sentence).
- Continue ascent to optimal altitude (build up weaker side of the argument).
- Cruise at optimal altitude, navigating bouts of turbulence in the process (assert stronger side of the argument, including counters to the points made earlier).
- Prepare for landing (produce an evaluation that explains why your chosen side of the argument is stronger).

While pupils are writing their paragraphs, mark their introductions (awarding five points for each of the bullet-point prompts) and write the scores on the board.

Stage 3: Landing. Ask each group to write a conclusion, using the prompts below:

- Instruct cabin crew to prepare for landing (restate answer to the question).
- Communicate with air-traffic control to negotiate an agreed landing slot (acknowledge weaker side of the argument).
- Complete flight with a smooth landing, revelling in your passengers' applause as you do so (explain why you've opted for your chosen conclusion).

While pupils are writing their conclusions, mark their main paragraphs (awarding 10 marks for each of the bullet-point prompts) and add to the totals from Stage 1. Mark the conclusions before the next lesson, when you can reveal the overall winner and undertake some peer assessment.

What you'll need to prepare in advance

- This is one of the most low-effort, high-impact lessons in the book. The main thing to do in advance is to ask pupils to prepare an essay plan for homework, so that in class they can focus more on practising writing skills than on knowledge recall.

- Produce some accompanying slides with prompts for each of the three stages. If you'd like to save time, you can adapt my presentation (available at www.the-writing-game.com).

Possible adaptations

1. If you're pressed for time, or if you'd prefer to focus on practising technique for individual paragraphs rather than whole essays, you could change the stages to the following:

- **Take-Off**: move towards maximal altitude by building up the weaker side of the argument.

- **Flight**: cruise at maximal altitude, navigating pockets of turbulence, by asserting the merits of the stronger side of the argument, unpicking problems with the weaker side as you do so.

- **Landing**: complete your flight with an end-of-paragraph evaluation explaining why your chosen line of argument is more persuasive.

2. If you have the technological capability for creating shared documents, you can provide live feedback to each group while they are writing.

3. If you're feeling really cheesy, you can give yourself the role of Air-Traffic Control, encouraging pupils to make radio contact with you if they have a phrasing or knowledge question.

Top tips
- Think carefully about the groups that pupils are working in. Sometimes you might want to group by attainment level, but at other times it can be useful to have mixed attainment groups.
- Encourage every member of each group to take responsibility for being the scribe in at least one of the stages.
- Challenge higher-attaining pupils to use complex target vocabulary.
- Use excerpts from the work produced for peer assessment or modelling activities in the next lesson. Again, if you're feeling particularly corny, you can call this Quality Control and ask pupils to mark each excerpt against a checklist of quality criteria.

Links to the evidence base

- Graham's (2018) finding that the most effective writing instructors create 'classroom writing communities' in which pupils frequently collaborate on low-stakes writing tasks.

- Wiliam's (2013) recommendation that tasks should be designed to elicit evidence of learning and lead to responsive teaching that addresses imperfections.

 # ESSAY TRIATHLON

This three-part lesson is one of my favourite ways of helping pupils to prepare for extended writing. It can work really well halfway through a topic for exploring an essay question that relates to recent content, later in a topic in place of a traditional end-of-unit essay, or as a revision activity.

Although they all use different themes, Essay Triathlon is essentially the same as The War of the Words (page 89) and Essay Jet (page 93). Using all three over the course of an academic year will ensure that your pupils practise the same skills repeatedly, while keeping things fresh and avoiding diminishing returns through activity fatigue.

LESSON PLAN

Starter

In pairs or threes, pupils must produce a list of words/phrases that they would expect to see in a Grade 8/9 or A*/A essay (adapt accordingly depending on the attainment profile of your class). Write these on the board, where they should remain for the duration of the lesson.

Main

Stage 1: Swim. Ask each group to write an introduction to the essay that they've planned in advance. Remind them of the component skills that you're trying to impart with the following prompts:

- Acquaint yourselves with the water conditions (define key terms).

- Demonstrate your own capabilities and test out your rivals (discuss a two-sided argument).

- Make a final surge so you can be first out of the water (direct your answer to the question, explaining why it's the most persuasive interpretation).

Stage 2: Cycle. Ask each group to write a main paragraph. Again, remind them of the component skills you'd like them to practise with the following prompts:

- On the uphill stage, allow your rivals to establish a slight lead, conserving enough of your own energy for the sprint finish (present the weaker side of the argument).

- As you come downhill and on to the flat, chip away at your rivals' lead and re-establish yourself as the front runner (present the stronger side of the argument).

- On the sprint finish, pull away from your rivals so you can be the first off your bike (produce an evaluation that explains why one side of the argument is more persuasive than the other).

While pupils are writing this section, mark their introductions (awarding five marks for each of the bullet-point prompts) and write the totals on the board.

Stage 3: Run. Ask each group to write a conclusion. Use the prompts below:

- Demonstrate your capability once more by extending your lead (answer the question).

- Show you have the versatility to beat your rivals on the running stage as well as in the water and on the bike (acknowledge the other side of the argument).

- Sprint to the finish (provide a final explanation for why your chosen argument is the most compelling).

While pupils are writing their conclusions, mark their main paragraphs (awarding 10 marks for each of the bullet-point prompts) and add to the totals from Stage 1. Mark the conclusions before the next lesson, when you can reveal the overall winner and undertake some peer assessment.

What you'll need to prepare in advance

- Again, this is one of the most low-effort, high-impact lessons in the book. The main thing to do in advance is to ask pupils to prepare an essay plan for homework, so that in class they can focus more on practising writing skills than on knowledge recall.

- Produce some accompanying slides with prompts for each of the three stages. If you'd like to save time, you can adapt my presentation (available at www.the-writing-game.com).

Possible adaptations

1. If you're pressed for time, or if you'd prefer to focus on practising technique for individual paragraphs rather than whole essays, you could change the stages to the following:

- **Swim**: get off to a good start by building up the weaker side of the argument.

- **Cycle**: extend your lead by asserting the stronger side of the argument.

- **Run**: secure your victory with an end-of-paragraph evaluation explaining why your chosen line of argument is more persuasive.

2. If you have the technological capability for creating shared documents, you can provide live feedback to each group while they are writing.

3. If you're feeling really cheesy, you can give each group an energy gel (real or imaginary), which they can use to ask for your help with a phrasing or knowledge question.

Top tips

- Award bonus points if teams use all the target vocabulary on the board, or if they manage to pull off a skill (like a balanced judgement) that you've been working on recently.

- Think carefully about the groups that pupils are working in. Sometimes you might want to group by attainment level, but at other times it can be useful to have mixed attainment groups.

- Encourage every member of each group to take responsibility for being the scribe in at least one of the stages.
- Challenge higher-attaining pupils to use complex target vocabulary.
- Use excerpts from the work produced for peer assessment or modelling activities in the next lesson.

Links to the evidence base

- Graham's (2018) finding that the most effective writing instructors create 'classroom writing communities' in which pupils frequently collaborate on low-stakes writing tasks.
- Wiliam's (2006) finding that tasks should be designed to elicit evidence of learning and lead to responsive teaching that addresses imperfections.

JEOPARDY

My take on the classic American TV game show is a useful whole-lesson activity to have up your sleeve. Equally applicable during a GCSE or A Level course, or as part of a revision programme, it provides opportunities for deliberate, sentence-level practice across a range of subject content and assessment criteria.

Warning: this one can become highly competitive, so make sure you bring your A game.

LESSON PLAN

Divide the class into groups of five or six pupils. Introduce the activity. Explain that sentences worth 100 points will be the most straightforward, with the requirements increasing in difficulty as the points on offer rise.

Ask each group to choose their first points challenge. You can adapt according to the demands of your subject, but as a guide I recommend the following levels of difficulty:

- 100 points: one sentence giving an accurate definition of a concept.

- 200 points: one sentence giving an accurate example supporting a pre-determined line of argument.

- 300 points: two sentences providing an example and an explanation of significance.

- 400 points: two sentences providing, with supporting evidence, an effective counter to a specified line of argument.

> • 500 points: three sentences outlining a two-sided argument and providing a justified judgement.
>
> Assess the efforts and decide whether each group has done enough to earn the points, crossing off any squares that have been completed on the Jeopardy board. Ask each group to choose their second points challenge.
>
> Repeat the process as many times as you see fit, keeping a running total on the board.

What you'll need to prepare in advance

Decide on the topic categories for each column of the Jeopardy board and then the challenges for each row. You can find a template at www.the-writing-game.com.

Possible adaptations

1. If you're worried that your pupils might struggle to fulfil the criteria for each level of difficulty, provide some model sentences that demonstrate what you're looking for. This will take a little longer to prepare, but it will leave them in no doubt as to what excellence looks like.

2. If you have a long lesson to fill, you could give teams the opportunity to 'steal' points from each other by writing a perfect sentence/pair of sentences when one group fails to meet the criteria needed to earn points.

3. You could add a peer-assessment element, asking each team to appraise another team's effort and make a recommendation on whether they should receive the points. Make sure you act as the ultimate arbiter to avoid bitter feuds!

Top tips

- Use a mini-whiteboard or a shared document facility so you can assess each group's sentences quickly.
- Draw attention to any particularly effective writing, asking pupils in other groups to evaluate its strengths.
- Assign pupils to teams that contain a mix of attainment levels. As well as providing a fair competition, this will enable the lower-attaining members of the class to learn from their higher-attaining peers.

Links to the evidence base

- Willingham's (2006) finding that the best learning happens when pupils are required to think about something that activates their prior knowledge.
- Graham's (2018) finding that group writing exercises are a hallmark of effective writing skill instruction.
- Wiliam and Thompson's (2007) recommendation that teachers should activate pupils as learning resources for each other.

WRITE-PAIR-SHARE

A variation on the old favourite Think-Pair-Share, this starter or plenary activity is an effective way of building your pupils' writing confidence, particularly in the early stages of the course or topic.

ACTIVITY OUTLINE

Working on their own at first, pupils write a series of sentences or a paragraph addressing a question relating to content that you've recently covered.

Once they've done this, ask them to work with a partner to produce an improved version. Then share with another pair, who provide feedback based on clearly defined criteria.

What you'll need to prepare in advance

A writing challenge and some criteria to guide the peer assessment.

Possible adaptations

1. You could combine Write-Pair-Share with Judgement Jenga (page 52) or Argument Tennis (page 59), asking each pair to produce a full, two-sided paragraph containing effective arguments and counter-arguments.

2. Provide live feedback by using a shared document facility or mini-whiteboards.

3. If you have time, expand the activity to Model-Write-Pair-Share, using a modelling exercise such as Basic, Better, Best (page 22) or Mark My Words (page 27).

Top tips

- Adjust your seating plan according to the particular needs of your pupils. You could either deliberately pair high-attaining pupils with lower-attaining peers, or group by attainment level. Don't just leave it to chance!

- Provide sentence frames to help your less-confident pupils use target language that satisfies your subject's assessment criteria.

Links to the evidence base

- Wiliam and Thompson's (2007) recommendation that teachers should activate pupils as learning resources for each other.

- Graham's (2018) finding that the most effective writing instructors create 'classroom writing communities' in which pupils frequently collaborate on low-stakes writing tasks.

THE GENERATION GAME

Far more than a homage to the hit TV show of my youth, this is a great starter or plenary activity that activates learners' prior knowledge and provides an opportunity for guided practice of key writing skills.

ACTIVITY OUTLINE

Divide the class into pairs or small groups. Using a preloaded word generator (find links to some that I've used at www.the-writing-game.com), instruct your pupils to write a sentence or mini-paragraph using the words and phrases generated.

For example, if you were teaching *Romeo and Juliet* to a GCSE English literature class, you might load the generator with the following words and phrases, from which three would be selected at random:

- conveys
- 'star-cross'd lovers'
- tragedy
- love
- feud

Discuss pupils' solutions as a class, working through a model if necessary. Repeat as many times as you see fit.

What you'll need to prepare in advance

Only the words and phrases to put into the generator. Make sure these contain target vocabulary or prompts for content (like examples, quotations or case studies) that you'd like to see in your pupils' essays.

Possible adaptations

1. If you have more time to fill, you could produce more words and phrases, and ask your pupils to write an entire paragraph.

2. You could combine The Generation Game with another activity like Judgement Day (page 30) or Paragraph Purgatory (page 33), asking pupils to assess each other's work against a set of clearly defined assessment criteria.

3. If you'd like to provide some scaffolding at an early stage of the GCSE or A Level course, you could use The Generation Game directly before a timed individual essay or group writing activity, challenging your pupils to use the selected words or phrases in their own work.

Top tip

Make sure you strike an appropriate balance between straightforward and complex vocabulary, so there's a degree of both support and challenge. You can obviously adapt this according to the profile of your cohort and the stage of the course that you've reached.

Link to the evidence base

Rosenshine's (2012) finding that the most effective teachers provide initial scaffolds for difficult tasks.

ROLE PLAY

As much as I'm an advocate of group writing exercises, I often find that the same voices dominate discussions over phrasing and argument formation. Role Play tries to mitigate this by assigning specific areas of responsibility to individual pupils. Use it either as a standalone task or in conjunction with another extended writing activity like The War of the Words (page 89), Essay Jet (page 93) or Essay Triathlon (page 97).

ACTIVITY OUTLINE

Divide the class into small groups and introduce the essay or short-answer question that you've chosen to focus on. Cast each group member in a different role. For example:

- The Scribe (responsible for writing and deciding how to phrase points).
- The Font of All Knowledge (responsible for supporting examples).
- The Analyst (responsible for explaining the significance of points).
- Mary, Mary, Quite Contrary (responsible for generating counter-arguments).
- The Judge (responsible for evaluations).

Sticking to these roles, pupils must write an introduction, main paragraph or conclusion in their groups.

What you'll need to prepare in advance

- Just make sure you've decided on the various roles that you want to assign.
- If you like, you can ask your pupils to prepare a paragraph or essay plan in advance, but you might decide that they would benefit from some on-the-spot generative recall.

Possible adaptations

1. If you'd like to fill all or most of a lesson, you could extend this activity to encompass an introduction, main paragraph *and* a conclusion, changing pupils' roles for each stage.

2. Alternatively, if you don't have lots of time to spare but would like to challenge your pupils to perform different roles, you could have a surprise reshuffle halfway through the activity, reassigning everyone's responsibilities.

3. You could cast your most confident and high-attaining pupils as teachers, asking them to provide live feedback to their group in the form of questions such as 'Which more recent example would be more relevant there?' and 'How could you counter that argument more effectively?'

Top tips

- Support your less confident pupils by providing sentence frames and some hints for relevant examples.
- Keep a copy of the work produced to use in future modelling exercises.

Link to the evidence base

Nestojko et al's (2014) finding that students who expect to have to impart knowledge and skills to others perform significantly better than those who don't.

LEVELLING UP

No, this isn't an activity sponsored by the Conservative Party. Levelling Up is an easy-to-implement, highly adaptable activity that, like Essay Doctors (page 118) and The News Room (page 121), facilitates deliberate practice of writing skills with increasing levels of difficulty. Although it can be tweaked to suit any stage of a unit or topic, I would suggest using it once a decent chunk of material has been covered; otherwise, the analysis and evaluation skills will be difficult to execute.

ACTIVITY OUTLINE

Working either in small groups or as individuals, pupils must complete the level 1 writing challenge. Once they've done so to your satisfaction, they can move on to level 2, then on to level 3 and beyond. For example:

- Level 1: write a sentence identifying an example of anti-immigration sentiment in France.

- Level 2: write two sentences explaining why 20th/21st-century immigration has challenged the concept of *laïcité*.

- Level 3: write two sentences outlining efforts to reconcile the desires of the immigrant population with the sentiments of the pro-assimilation lobby.

- Level 4: write a short paragraph arguing that the concept of *laïcité* should be reconsidered.

- Level 5: write a conclusion weighing up whether you feel France should do more to atone for its colonial past.

What you'll need to prepare in advance

Just the levels. As ever, ensure that there's an appropriate level of challenge, and try to address some topic areas and writing skills that your pupils tend to find difficult.

Possible adaptations

1. You could add a retrieval element by including at least one level based on a previous topic.

2. Stretch your highest-attaining pupils by imposing constraints on the evidence and language they can use, challenging them to complete each level without using certain common sentence constructions and examples.

Top tip

When providing feedback on why a pupil/group hasn't yet qualified to move up a level, ask questions like 'Why do you think your analysis isn't as good as it could be?' and 'What do you think that sentence is lacking at the moment?' rather than simply diagnosing the problems for them.

Link to the evidence base

Rosenshine's (2012) finding that the most effective teachers provide initial scaffolds for difficult tasks.

PARA-TROOPERS

As outlined in the introduction to this book, research on writing skill development – and on effective pedagogy more generally – is unambiguous in emphasising the need for mastery over specific parts of a skill before attempting to master the whole. This makes perfect sense: it's why a goalkeeper will not confine their practice regime to match scenarios, but will instead practise fielding crosses, saving penalties and stopping free kicks in isolation.

The demands of essay writing may vary across different academic disciplines, but the importance of a well-constructed paragraph is a constant. Para-Troopers aims to guide pupils towards mastering this skill, providing opportunities for scaffolding, deliberate practice and peer assessment along the way.

ACTIVITY OUTLINE

Using a pre-planned essay/short-answer question, introduce pupils to their mission: to produce a paragraph that has military-level precision.

Outline the equipment they will need and the core objectives of their mission. For example:

Equipment

- Four quotations (two from *Othello* and two from *Jane Eyre*).
- Two accompanying comparative points.
- Two critical interpretations.
- Their own judgement on whether the two texts can be described as tales of jealousy.

Core objectives

- Produce a clear, consistent line of argument that is signposted at the beginning and end of the paragraph.
- Demonstrate awareness of both sides of the argument.
- Provide evidence of their ability to analyse language.
- Assess the validity of critical interpretations.

Working in small groups, pupils have to undertake their mission. Once the paragraphs have been completed, swap them between groups and ask pupils to carry out a review of each other's missions.

What you'll need to prepare in advance

A list of the equipment and core objectives that your para-troopers will need to complete their mission.

Possible adaptations

1. If you have access to shared documents, cast yourself as Mission Control and provide live feedback to each group while they are writing.
2. Add some differentiation by subtly providing groups with different equipment and core objectives, depending on their recent attainment.
3. If you're confident that your pupils have already developed a proficient understanding of how to construct effective paragraphs, challenge them to generate the lists of equipment and core objectives. Discuss as a class and address any misconceptions that arise.

Top tip

Ask your pupils to prepare an essay plan in advance. This will ensure that their cognitive processing can be focused on how best to execute the writing skills that you're trying to impart, rather than on knowledge recall.

Links to the evidence base

- Troia's (2014) finding that providing instruction on paragraph structure is a hallmark of effective writing pedagogy.
- Khattab's (2015) finding that students with higher aspirations and expectations perform better than those with lower aspirations and expectations.

TOUGH LOVE

I fully appreciate that there are plenty of activities in this book whose names you'd rather not use when introducing them to your pupils: Mary, Mary, Quite Contrary (page 57) or All Things Write and Beautiful (page 128) might not go down too well with a stony-faced, cynical bunch of sixth-formers.

But Tough Love is the one activity in this book whose name you *cannot* reveal to your pupils, because it gives away the cunning deception at its heart. It's probably best used as a revision activity, or in the final stages of a GCSE or A Level course, although it could work well with a high-attaining group at an earlier point.

ACTIVITY OUTLINE

Working in pairs or small groups, pupils must write down a list of their favourite connectives, sentence constructions and other target language for essays in your subject. Discuss their lists as a class, writing a master list on the board/screen.

Then introduce an essay/short-answer question relating to material that you've recently taught or revised, creating the impression that the pupils will be using the language on the board to help them write a paragraph. But, just before they start writing, reveal that they have to do so without using *any* of the language on the board.

Once they've finished writing, discuss how they found solutions to the constraints you imposed on them. Add the new connectives, constructions and target language to the list on the board, asking pupils to copy down each other's solutions.

What you'll need to prepare in advance

Nothing, except perhaps a thick armour to withstand all the sighs, groans and glares that pupils will direct at you once you reveal the true nature of the exercise.

Possible adaptations

1. Incorporate some peer assessment afterwards, asking pupils to provide feedback on each other's paragraphs. If you choose this option, you might want to combine Tough Love with another activity like Paragraph Purgatory (page 33) or Para-Troopers (page 112), so there's a clear set of criteria for judging each paragraph's effectiveness.

2. You could tweak the activity slightly by asking pupils to produce a list of their favourite/best-known examples/quotations on a certain topic or text, and then banning them from using those.

Top tip

Save the paragraphs your pupils produce for use in other activities like Basic, Better, Best (page 22) and Para-Medics (page 138).

Link to the evidence base

Rosenshine's (2012) finding that 'students need extensive, successful, independent practice in order for skills and knowledge to become automatic'.

Redrafting

ESSAY DOCTORS

One of our most important tasks as teachers is to identify the content and skills that our pupils are most likely to find challenging, then design learning activities that get ahead of the problem.

Essay Doctors aims to address misconceptions before they have fully taken root in learners' minds, by providing a range of opportunities for evaluating knowledge recall, explicitly debunking misconceptions and practising key writing skills. The activity works well towards the end of a unit or topic, allowing you to build in some retrieval practice from earlier lessons while preparing pupils for an extended piece of writing.

In each of the tasks, pupils are required to diagnose the problems with the excerpt and then treat them by rewriting the affected section or sections.

LESSON PLAN

Provide a handout containing five excerpts answering an essay question that you've recently considered. Working in pairs or threes, pupils consider each excerpt in turn and only move on to the next one once they've produced their diagnosis and treatment.

1. Medical student

At this initial stage, ask pupils to diagnose and treat a relatively basic knowledge problem.

2. Junior doctor

This stage can be a little more complex, perhaps combining less basic knowledge problems with a lack of analysis.

---

3. Registrar

You should now start to test your pupils' ability to spot and deal with poor evaluation.

4. Consultant

This is a good opportunity to produce a near-perfect paragraph with a couple of minor errors, testing your pupils' attention to detail and understanding of the key writing skills that you're attempting to impart.

5. Chief medical officer

Building on the skills tested in the previous stage, in order to qualify as chief medical officers, pupils should be able to diagnose and treat minor problems with knowledge, analysis and evaluation.

Review each diagnosis and discuss possible treatments as a whole class at the end of the lesson.

What you'll need to prepare in advance

- This is one of the more time-consuming activities in the book, so it's definitely not one to pick if you only have 20 minutes to plan your lesson. You'll need to write or source five excerpts from an essay that relates to something you've been studying recently, making sure there are diagnosable problems with each excerpt, as described in the lesson plan. You can find the template at www. the-writing-game.com.

- Once you've created one set of excerpts, you can reuse them in subsequent years, adapting as you see fit.

Possible adaptations

1. If you're worried that the diagnosis part of each task might be too challenging for some of your pupils, you could provide a scaffold by telling them what type of problem each excerpt is suffering from: inaccurate knowledge, poor analysis, insufficient evaluation, etc. Likewise, if you're worried that the treatment part of the tasks

might be too challenging, you could provide sentence frames to help pupils construct more effective analyses and evaluations.

2. This activity can also work well as a homework task, providing a stimulus for discussion in the next lesson.

3. If you have time and you're looking to jazz up your feedback, you could even personalise the tasks for each pupil, using excerpts from their most recent essays and asking them to diagnose and treat problems with their own work.

Top tips

- You know your pupils' strengths and weaknesses better than anyone, so make sure your excerpts contain examples of common issues in their written work. If you know they find it difficult to justify their judgements, for example, include a poorly justified judgement in at least one of the passages.

- In your questioning, be sure to probe your pupils' understanding of *why* the issues contained within each excerpt constitute examples of ineffective writing.

- Challenge high-attaining pupils by imposing constraints on the language they can use in their treatments. For example, ask them to justify their judgements without using 'because', 'since' or 'as'.

Links to the evidence base

- Rosenshine's (2012) finding that the most effective modelling must engage pupils' cognitive processing, requiring them to evaluate why an example is effective.

- Rosenshine's (2012) emphasis on the importance of explicitly addressing common misconceptions.

- Graham's (2018) finding that the most effective writing instructors create 'classroom writing communities' in which pupils frequently collaborate on low-stakes writing tasks.

- Wiliam's (2006) finding that peer and self-assessment are crucial to maximising pupils' progress.

THE NEWS ROOM

Like Upcycling (page 35) and Essay Doctors (page 118), this whole-lesson sequence of activities entails a range of scaffolded writing tasks of increasing difficulty, which can easily be adapted to suit the needs of your pupils. It's particularly well suited to the final stages of a unit or topic, providing a blend of knowledge recall, deliberate practice and feedback opportunities that will sharpen your pupils' minds before a more formal assessment. This activity turns your classroom into a newspaper office, with each pupil beginning as a trainee journalist and then working their way up through the ranks.

LESSON PLAN

Provide pupils with a handout containing five writing tasks relating to recent material. Working in pairs or threes, they must complete each task in turn, only moving on to the next level of the newspaper once their work has been signed off by the proprietor (you).

1. Work experience

At this initial stage, ask pupils to write a simple sentence/set of sentences outlining some basic knowledge points.

2. Reporter

Test pupils' ability to report facts in an accurate, detailed manner by asking them to produce a developed point that is supported by evidence.

3. Correspondent

Start to test your pupils' analysis skills by asking them to construct a line of argument, supported by evidence and explanation.

4. Columnist

Increase the level of difficulty by tasking your pupils with writing a one-sided paragraph, building up the argument as persuasively as possible, with evidence and analysis to support a range of points.

5. Editor

Finally, ask your pupils to produce a balanced, two-sided paragraph that reaches a clear, justified conclusion on which side of the argument is most convincing.

What you'll need to prepare in advance

The series of graduated writing tasks that your pupils will need to complete in order to move up the newspaper's hierarchy. You can find a template at www.the-writing-game.com.

Possible adaptations

1. Add a 'sub-editor' stage in which pupils are required to edit each other's writing. Alternatively, you could prepare a flawed paragraph in advance, using previous pupils' work in order to save time.

2. Incentivise the use of target language and skills by producing a list of features that will improve newspaper sales or generate clicks – for instance, multi-skill sentences, nuanced lines of argument and cross-topic examples.

3. Challenge your highest-attaining pupils by producing a list of house style guidelines that prohibit the use of particularly common words and sentence constructions.

Top tips

- When discussing whether each group is ready to move on to the next task, ask questions that engage pupils' self-evaluation skills. For example, 'Why do you think that final sentence is particularly effective?' or 'Why do you think I'd like you to rewrite this opening section?'

- Use either a shared document facility or mini-whiteboards to enable you to assess each group's work as efficiently as possible.
- Begin your next lesson with a peer-assessment task (similar to Basic, Better, Best on page 22) that requires pupils to choose the best paragraph produced in the 'Editor' stage. As ever, make sure you save all the paragraphs for use in future activities like Essay Doctors (page 118) and All Things Write and Beautiful (page 128).

Links to the evidence base

- Graham's (2018) finding that the most effective writing instructors create 'classroom writing communities' in which pupils frequently collaborate on low-stakes writing tasks.
- Rosenshine's (2012) recommendation that teachers should provide initial scaffolds for difficult tasks.
- Wiliam's (2013) finding that tasks should be designed to elicit evidence of learning and lead to responsive teaching that addresses imperfections.

THE REFINERY

This is a great starter or plenary activity that has the dual benefit of helping pupils to review their knowledge and practise their writing.

ACTIVITY OUTLINE

Using either a projector or a whiteboard, write a deliberately error-strewn paragraph answering a question that you've been considering recently in class. Make sure you combine knowledge errors with poor phrasing.

Working in pairs or threes, pupils must refine the paragraph, writing a fresh version that is free from the problems afflicting yours.

Review their paragraphs either while they complete the next lesson task or after the lesson, then provide whole-class feedback.

What you'll need to prepare in advance

If you're comfortable producing an error-strewn paragraph on the spot then you don't need to prepare anything in advance. If you'd rather not have the pressure of doing it live, you'll need to write one before the lesson and either project it, copy it out on the board or include it on a handout.

Possible adaptations

1. If you'd like to provide a scaffold for your less confident pupils, you could produce a series of sentence frames for them to use when refining the paragraph.

2. If you'd like to stretch your more confident, higher-attaining pupils, you could challenge them to produce a refined version

that contains none of the same vocabulary or examples that you included in the original version.

3. You could make this into a retrieval activity by writing a paragraph on a past topic.

4. If you're particularly impressed with one of the refined paragraphs, you could use it for a modelling exercise in a future lesson (such as Basic, Better, Best on page 22 or Paragraph Purgatory on page 33).

Top tip

When choosing which errors to make in your paragraph, try to highlight common mistakes made by your pupils in order to satisfy Rosenshine's (2012) recommendation of explicitly addressing recurrent misconceptions.

Link to the evidence base

Troia's (2014) recommendation that teachers should provide activities in which students compare and contrast superior exemplars with inferior ones.

THE SUBS' DESK

Inspired by my professionally pedantic father, who used to work as a newspaper sub-editor, The Subs' Desk incentivises attention to detail while reviewing pupils' knowledge. A longer, adapted version of Sentence Saviours (page 130), this activity works equally well as a starter or as a plenary.

ACTIVITY OUTLINE

Using either a lesson handout or a projector, ask your pupils to read through a flawed paragraph relating to material that they've recently learned.

Working in pairs or threes, pupils must identify the errors and then perform the role of sub-editor by correcting each one. Discuss their solutions as a class.

What you'll need to prepare in advance

Like Sentence Saviours, this is an ideal activity for time-pressed teachers: all you need to prepare is a paragraph containing some knowledge and phrasing errors. If you're super-busy, you could use a paragraph written by a past pupil.

Possible adaptations

1. You could incorporate The Subs' Desk into a feedback lesson, using an anonymised paragraph written by a member of the class.

2. Alternatively, you could employ it as a retrieval activity, using a paragraph relating to content covered some weeks or months earlier.

3. If you're looking to fill an entire lesson, perhaps in preparation for an upcoming assessment, you could pair The Subs' Desk with

another activity like Para-Troopers (page 112), using it as a starter activity to stimulate discussion about what makes an effective paragraph, before asking your pupils to complete some deliberate practice.

Top tip

Make sure that the paragraph you use contains some common misconceptions or skill errors. Addressing these before a more formal assessment is a great way of boosting your pupils' long-term retention.

Link to the evidence base

Rosenshine's (2012) finding that the most effective teachers explicitly address common misconceptions.

ALL THINGS WRITE AND BEAUTIFUL

The need to design activities that explicitly address learners' misconceptions is clearly expressed in the evidence base on effective pedagogy, as well as in research on effective writing instruction. A close relative of The Refinery (page 124) and Para-Medics (page 138), All Things Write and Beautiful seeks to do just this, while also providing an opportunity for scaffolded writing practice.

Although it can be adapted to suit any stage of a scheme of work, I would recommend using this activity roughly halfway through a unit of study so knowledge gaps are remedied before they become rooted in your pupils' mental schema.

ACTIVITY OUTLINE

Ask your pupils to consider the constituent parts of a 'beautiful' paragraph. Briefly discuss as a class, addressing any misconceptions that arise.

Give your pupils an error-strewn paragraph answering a question that relates to recent material. Working in pairs or threes, pupils must edit the paragraph to create their own version that is both accurate and well presented.

Provide whole-class feedback on the problems affecting the original paragraph and the effectiveness of each group's corrected versions.

What you'll need to prepare in advance

The paragraph that you'd like your pupils to edit. As ever, the most efficient way of preparing this is to use a paragraph written by a previous pupil or group of pupils, in either an end-of-topic essay or a collaborative writing task like Snakes and Ladders (page 82) or Essay Triathlon (page 97).

Possible adaptations

1. Using either mini-whiteboards or a shared document facility, provide live feedback to each group while they are writing up their corrected versions.

2. Challenge your highest-attaining pupils by giving them a list of particularly 'beautiful' features that you'd like them to include, such as multi-skill sentences, cross-topic examples and nuanced lines of argument (adapt as appropriate for your subject).

3. Use the paragraphs produced as the basis for a peer-assessment task like Basic, Better, Best (page 22) or Paragraph Purgatory (page 33), either directly after All Things Write and Beautiful or at the beginning of the next lesson.

Top tip

Although you can use a previous pupil's work as the basis, make a few choice edits in order to ensure the activity addresses the skills or knowledge that your pupils are finding most challenging.

Link to the evidence base

Graham's (2018) recommendation that teachers should use group writing activities to facilitate deliberate, guided practice.

SENTENCE SAVIOURS

A shorter, adapted version of The Subs' Desk (page 126), Sentence Saviours is a super-quick plenary task that reviews pupils' knowledge and gives them a chance to practise their writing.

ACTIVITY OUTLINE

Using either a lesson handout or a projector, provide a series of flawed sentences relating to content you've recently covered. Through discussion with the whole class, model how to save one of the sentences.

Working in pairs or groups of three, pupils must save each sentence by eradicating the errors they've identified. Discuss their solutions as a class.

What you'll need to prepare in advance

This is a great activity for busy teachers. All you need to do in advance is produce a series of 3-5 flawed sentences, taking care to include a range of knowledge and skill errors.

Possible adaptations

1. You could incorporate Sentence Saviours into a feedback lesson, using anonymised sentences written by members of the class. This is an effective way of addressing common misconceptions and, to borrow Tom Sherrington's (2019) phrase, encouraging pupils to 'say it again, better'.

2. If you'd like to increase the level of challenge for your highest-attaining pupils, you could encourage them to save each sentence without using any of the words that appear in the original versions.

3. If you'd like to offer additional support to lower-attaining pupils, provide a few sentence frames on the board or handout.

Top tip

Challenge your highest-attaining pupils by including at least one near-perfect sentence that contains only a very minor, hard-to-spot flaw.

Link to the evidence base

Rosenshine's (2012) finding that the most effective teachers explicitly address common misconceptions.

SIMPLES

This quick and easy activity tries to solve the opposite problem to The Vicar of Glibly (page 55): overcomplication. I'm sure every humanities teacher has taught pupils who can't help but tie themselves in knots with excessively complex, unclear phrasing.

But no matter how frequently we tell them to simplify their writing and to shorten their sentences, they are unlikely to make progress without opportunities for deliberate practice based on models of excellence. A versatile starter or plenary task, Simples aims to do just that.

ACTIVITY OUTLINE

Using a presentation or a handout, provide your pupils with 3-5 poorly phrased, overcomplicated sentences relating to recently learned material.

Model how to simplify at least one of the sentences, remembering to probe your pupils' understanding of *why* the rewritten version is more effective than the original.

Working in pairs or threes, pupils must simplify the remaining sentences.

What you'll need to prepare in advance

A series of 3-5 excessively complex, poorly phrased sentences, with at least one simplified solution to use as a model.

Possible adaptations

1. If you have time, you could beef up this activity by using entire paragraphs rather than self-contained sentences.

2. If you're able to use shared documents, you can provide live feedback, asking questions like 'How could you make that clause even clearer?' and 'How could you add an example to that sentence without compromising the clarity?'

3. If you think this activity is unnecessary for some of your higher-attaining pupils, you could run it in conjunction with The Vicar of Glibly, enabling differentiation by task based on each pupil's particular needs.

Top tip

Support your less-confident pupils by providing some sentence frames to aid their redrafting.

Link to the evidence base

Troia's (2014) recommendation that teachers should use activities in which students compare and contrast superior exemplars with inferior ones.

DRAFT PUNK

One of the cheesiest names for one of my favourite activities. Draft Punk is an easy way of testing your pupils' subject knowledge, reintroducing them to writing practice and improving their understanding of assessment criteria. It can work well as a preparatory activity before an end-of-topic essay, as retrieval practice, or as an informal way of consolidating learning halfway through a unit.

ACTIVITY OUTLINE

In pairs or threes, pupils must produce a paragraph relating to recently covered material.

Once they've all finished, ask them to pass their effort on to another group, who then have responsibility for improving their paragraph. Ask those groups to pass their paragraphs on to another group, who must make further improvements.

Collect the paragraphs at the end of the activity and provide whole-class feedback during the next lesson.

What you'll need to prepare in advance

Here's one of the best things about this activity: absolutely no preparation is needed. You might want to ask your pupils to plan an essay or a paragraph in advance, or you might decide that they would benefit from some generative recall during the lesson.

Possible adaptations

1. If you're looking to challenge your pupils a little more, you could turn this into an individual activity rather than a group one.

2. If you're able to use shared documents, you can provide live feedback, asking questions like 'How could you add another example to support your first point?' and 'How could you address the question more directly in your judgement?'

3. If you're pressed for time, you could ask each pupil to produce an initial draft for homework and then begin the activity with the first round of improvements.

Top tip

Support your less-confident pupils by providing some sentence frames to aid their redrafting.

Link to the evidence base

Wiliam's (2006) finding that peer and self-assessment are crucial to maximising pupils' progress.

REPHRASE ROULETTE

This is a great starter or plenary task that can be used at any stage of a unit to test pupils' knowledge and skills across a range of subject content and assessment objectives. Like its close relative, Sentence Saviours (page 130), Rephrase Roulette is very adaptable according to the particular strengths and weaknesses of your cohort.

ACTIVITY OUTLINE

Spin a roulette wheel on a PowerPoint presentation (see www.the-writing-game.com for my version). Depending on whether the dial lands on red or black, ask your pupils to work individually or in pairs/ small groups to rephrase a sentence/mini-paragraph that you've prepared in advance.

Discuss their solutions as a class, working through a model if necessary. Repeat as many times as you see fit.

What you'll need to prepare in advance

Download the roulette wheel from www.the-writing-game.com to save time, then produce 3-5 flawed sentences or mini-paragraphs that include a range of knowledge and skill errors. You could use past pupils' work to save time.

Possible adaptations

1. You could include Rephrase Roulette in a feedback lesson, using anonymised excerpts from your class's most recent essays and asking pupils to rephrase them.

2. Add a retrieval element by including at least one sentence or mini-paragraph relating to an earlier topic.

3. Incentivise high performance by formulating a scoring system. For example, completing an accurate solution could be worth £10,000 (make this 10,000 points if you're worried about encouraging gambling!), while including a detailed example or a multi-skill sentence could be worth £20,000.

Top tip

Adapt the activity according to your pupils' strengths and weaknesses. If you know they particularly struggle with forming evaluations or analysis, include a heavier weighting of these skills and produce a model to help them.

Link to the evidence base

Troia's (2014) recommendation that teachers should use activities in which students compare and contrast superior exemplars with inferior ones.

PARA-MEDICS

A shorter, spin-off version of Essay Doctors (page 118), Para-Medics is a versatile starter or plenary activity. It provides numerous opportunities for addressing common misconceptions, highlighting frequent skill and technique errors, and practising writing in a low-stakes environment.

ACTIVITY OUTLINE

Divide the class into small groups. Provide each group with a copy of an 'injured' paragraph, asking them to identify its various mistakes and shortcomings.

Discuss the issues with the paragraph as a class, making sure you explain why its 'injuries' constitute flaws. For example, 'The opening sentence only addresses half the question, which limits AO3 marks' and 'That long sentence should be split up into shorter sentences in order to explain the quotations more clearly for AO2 marks'.

What you'll need to prepare in advance

A paragraph containing a range of knowledge, skill and phrasing errors. It's best if this is deliberately constructed to include some of the most common problems that appear in your pupils' work on the topic in question. If you're pressed for time, you can always use an anonymised version of a paragraph written by a previous pupil, but make sure you select one carefully to maximise the activity's impact.

Possible adaptations

1. If you have plenty of lesson time to fill, add a peer-marking exercise afterwards, giving pupils the chance to critique each other's corrections.

2. Alternatively, if you don't have lots of time to spare, ask your pupils to carry out the diagnosis stage in pairs. After briefly discussing the paragraph's problems as a class, you can ask them to complete the treatment (corrections) for homework.

3. Differentiate the task by organising pupils into attainment-based groups and providing each group with a different paragraph. The lower-attaining pupils could be given a paragraph with lots of basic knowledge and technique errors, while the higher-attaining pupils could be given a near-perfect paragraph containing only a few minor errors.

Top tips

- Keep a copy of the work produced to use in future modelling exercises.
- In your next lesson, provide whole-class feedback on the strengths and weaknesses of the treated paragraphs.

Link to the evidence base

Graham's (2018) finding that the most effective writing instructors create 'classroom writing communities' in which pupils frequently collaborate on low-stakes writing tasks.

RUMBLE IN THE JUMBLE

I'll hold up my fists here: this is one of the less creative activities contained in this book. But although Rumble in the Jumble is ridiculously simple, it can be a really effective starter or plenary that aids pupils' recall, close reading and writing skills.

ACTIVITY OUTLINE

Divide the class into small groups. Provide each one with a copy of a jumbled-up exemplar paragraph from an essay relating to recently covered content.

Ask each group to reorder the paragraph until it is an exemplar again. Discuss their solutions as a class.

What you'll need to prepare in advance

Only the jumbled-up paragraph. Rather than writing one yourself, I suggest using an old paragraph typed by a former pupil. Anonymise it, then change the sentence order so that it become unrecognisable.

Possible adaptations

1. Particularly if you teach a language, or if you have lots of pupils for whom English isn't their first language, you can think about jumbling up the word order *within* some sentences, encouraging your pupils to think about correct grammar as well as argument formation.

2. Rather than using an exemplar paragraph, you could combine this activity with The Subs' Desk (page 126), asking your pupils to reorder *and* redraft a deliberately messy paragraph.

Top tip

When discussing how to organise a paragraph correctly with the whole class, make sure you probe your pupils' understanding of *why* it's best to form arguments in certain ways – for example, why it might be better to propose a weaker line of argument before putting forward a stronger line of argument.

Link to the evidence base

Troia's (2014) finding that providing instruction on paragraph structure is a hallmark of effective writing pedagogy.

Feedback

⧗⧗⧗ THE FEEDBACK LOOP

This isn't an activity so much as an approach to feedback. Since developing The Feedback Loop several years ago, I've found it an effective way of requiring pupils to engage in detailed reflections on their work, in line with findings by the likes of Wiliam (2006) and Willingham (2006), as well as the recommendations of writing instruction scholars such as Graham (2018), Troia (2014) and Hayes (2012).

A word of warning: most pupils will absolutely hate it initially, because it represents a departure from the approach taken by almost all their teachers for almost all their schooling. But, in my experience, they come to understand its merits as it becomes more familiar.

The Feedback Loop
Practise-Write-Reflect-Repeat

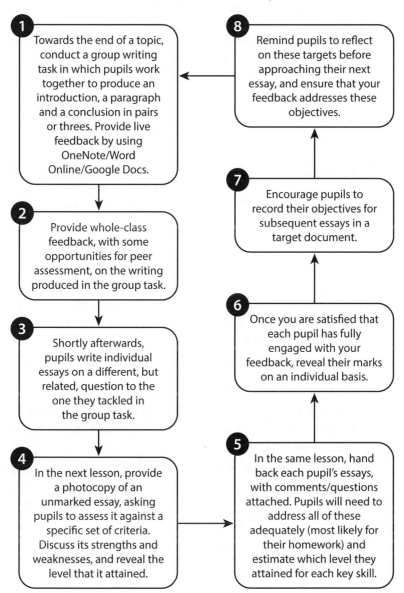

1 Towards the end of a topic, conduct a group writing task in which pupils work together to produce an introduction, a paragraph and a conclusion in pairs or threes. Provide live feedback by using OneNote/Word Online/Google Docs.

2 Provide whole-class feedback, with some opportunities for peer assessment, on the writing produced in the group task.

3 Shortly afterwards, pupils write individual essays on a different, but related, question to the one they tackled in the group task.

4 In the next lesson, provide a photocopy of an unmarked essay, asking pupils to assess it against a specific set of criteria. Discuss its strengths and weaknesses, and reveal the level that it attained.

5 In the same lesson, hand back each pupil's essays, with comments/questions attached. Pupils will need to address all of these adequately (most likely for their homework) and estimate which level they attained for each key skill.

6 Once you are satisfied that each pupil has fully engaged with your feedback, reveal their marks on an individual basis.

7 Encourage pupils to record their objectives for subsequent essays in a target document.

8 Remind pupils to reflect on these targets before approaching their next essay, and ensure that your feedback addresses these objectives.

Possible adaptations

1. Particularly if you're at an early stage of the course with a GCSE or A Level set, and if none of your pupils has written an essay that's a suitable model, you might wish to produce an exemplar paragraph or essay yourself. Although this is time-consuming, it can be well worth doing: it sharpens your own writing skills while ensuring that your pupils have a clear understanding of what excellence entails.

2. You could begin the feedback lesson with an activity like Sentence Saviours (page 130) or Rephrase Roulette (page 136), asking your pupils to improve anonymised excerpts from their peers' essays.

3. If your pupils are familiar with the marking criteria (which they should be after an essay or two), ask them to read through their own essay and guess the mark it has received before they start correcting it.

Top tips

- Wherever possible, mark using open questions that will engage your pupils' cognitive processing skills. For example, 'How might you improve this final sentence?' and 'What's missing from this introduction?'

- Encourage your pupils to keep a record of the targets that arise from each of their essays, perhaps using Target Zone (page 40) or Top Trumps (page 42). My mantra, which always provokes a few raised eyebrows, is that they should be aiming to make *better* mistakes each time they write, rather than simply repeating the same errors.

- When discussing the model essay, refer back to the language used in previous writing skill activities, such as the concepts of the Evaluation Nation and Oversell Hell from the Judgement Day activity (page 30).

- Keep soft copies of some pupils' essays to use in future activities such as Basic, Better, Best (page 22) and Paragraph Purgatory (page 33).

Links to the evidence base

- Graham's (2018) finding that the most effective writing instructors create 'classroom writing communities' in which pupils frequently collaborate on low-stakes writing tasks.
- Wiliam's (2013) finding that tasks should be designed to elicit evidence of learning and lead to responsive teaching that addresses imperfections.
- Holdsworth et al's (2018) conclusion that 'failure is a central part of learning, but its associated connotations need to be reconceptualised as a learning opportunity'.
- Wiliam's (2013) maxim that 'feedback should be more work for the recipient than the donor'.

FEEDBACK BINGO

Do you ever feel your whole-class feedback after essays fails to receive the amount of engagement and interest it deserves? I often get the impression that my comments are like the trailers or credits at either side of a much-anticipated movie: an unnecessary sideshow that's of peripheral importance when compared with the main event.

Feedback Bingo attempts to solve this problem while providing opportunities for generative recall and self-reflection. I tend to use it after an end-of-topic timed essay, but it would work equally well in the lesson after a group writing exercise like The War of the Words (page 89), Essay Jet (page 93) or Essay Triathlon (page 97).

ACTIVITY OUTLINE

Working in pairs or threes, pupils have to write down a list of five words or phrases they think you're likely to mention as part of your whole-class feedback. (Make sure they are all technical or subject-specific words/phrases; there's nothing to be gained if they try to game the system by writing down five common conjunctions.)

As you deliver your whole-class feedback, pupils tick off each word or phrase on their list. The first group to tick off their whole list shouts 'Bingo!' and is awarded a merit (or the equivalent in your school's reward system).

What you'll need to prepare in advance

Nothing extra: just the whole-class feedback that you'd usually deliver after an essay or group writing exercise.

Possible adaptation

You could combine this with a modelling activity like Basic, Better, Best (page 22) or Paragraph Purgatory (page 33), asking your pupils to guess which words or phrases you're likely to mention when discussing their work.

Top tip

Once you've finished the whole-class feedback, devote some time to checking your students' understanding of *why* each of the words or phrases on their bingo card are important components of essay technique.

Link to the evidence base

Willingham's (2006) finding that the best learning happens when pupils are required to think about something that activates their prior knowledge.

ACKNOWLEDGEMENTS

At the end of a book extolling the benefits of group writing, it's only fitting that I should take a moment to acknowledge the contributions of the cast of characters who have enabled me to realise this lifelong dream.

On the operational side, I've benefited enormously from the sage advice of Jonathan Barnes and Isla McMillan at John Catt Educational. And the book simply wouldn't have happened without Alex Sharratt's willingness to take a punt on an aspiring teacher-author with just 92 Twitter followers.

As the book evolved from a concept into a manuscript, I welcomed the critical eye of colleagues past and present: two fine economists, Gareth Matthews and David Beggs; a pair of excellent historians, Holly Partridge and Jonathan Dixon; and a religious guru and all-round *lekker oke*, Jarrod Taylor.

Steve Graham's research has helped to develop my understanding of the evidence base on effective writing instruction, and I'm so grateful that he agreed to write the foreword to the book. I hope this project enables his crucial research to reach a wider audience.

I have already mentioned my parents in the introduction, but while they have passed on some of their extensive knowledge about writing to me, that contribution pales into insignificance when compared with the wider impact they have made on my life. From my very first breath, they have been unstinting in their love (even when sorely tested by my haircuts and Maths results), boundless in their generosity and inspirational beyond measure. I will never be able to thank them enough.

If my parents have always boosted my confidence, my siblings have never missed an opportunity to cut me back down to size, but I'm equally thankful for all they have done for me throughout my childhood and my adult life thus far.

I owe a huge debt of gratitude to my employers present and past, Hampton School and Uppingham School, for encouraging my desire to investigate the science and theory underpinning education, and for investing great faith in me at every turn.

Finally, even though she is sitting next to me as I write this, I offer my heartfelt thanks to my fiancée, Harriet Oliphant, every bit as excellent a teacher as she is a housemate and best friend. She was the first person to humour my nascent idea for a book, then the first person to wade through a very messy first draft, and she is always the first person to pick me up in times of difficulty. That she was loyal enough to mirror my refusal to acknowledge the total lunacy of attempting to write a book at the same time as completing a master's, buying a flat and organising a wedding is testament to how supportive she is.

REFERENCES

Black, P, and Wiliam, D. (1998) 'Assessment and classroom learning', *Assessment in Education: Principles, Policy & Practice*, 5:1, 7-74

Black, P, Harrison, C, Lee, C, Marshall, B, and Wiliam, D. (2003) *Assessment for Learning: putting it into practice*, Open University Press

Black, P, Harrison, C, Lee, C, Marshall, B, and Wiliam, D. (2004) 'Working inside the Black Box: Assessment for Learning in the classroom', *Phi Delta Kappan*, 86:1, 8-21

Duin, AH, and Graves, MF. (1987) 'Intensive vocabulary instruction as a prewriting technique', *Reading Research Quarterly*, 22:3, 311-330

Graham, S, and Perin, D. (2007a) *Writing Next: effective strategies to improve writing of adolescents in middle and high schools*, Carnegie Corporation of New York

Graham, S, and Perin, D. (2007b) 'A meta-analysis of writing instruction for adolescent students', *Journal of Educational Psychology*, 99:3, 445-476

Graham, S, McKeown, D, Kiuhara, S, and Harris, KR. (2012) 'A meta-analysis of writing instruction for students in the elementary grades', *Journal of Educational Psychology*, 104:4, 879-896

Graham, S, Harris, KR, and Santangelo, T. (2015) 'Research-based writing practices and the Common Core: meta-analysis and meta-synthesis', *The Elementary School Journal*, 115:4, 498-522

Graham, S. (2018) 'A revised writer(s)-within-community model of writing', *Educational Psychologist*, 53:4, 258-279

Graham, S, and Harris, KR. (2019) 'Evidence-based practices in writing' in Graham, S, MacArthur, CA, and Hebert, M (eds), *Best Practices in Writing Instruction* (third edition), Guilford Press

Harris, KR, Graham, S, Mason, LH, and Friedlander, B. (2008) *Powerful Writing Strategies for all Students*, Brookes

Hattie, J, and Timperley, H. (2007) 'The power of feedback', *Review of Educational Research*, 77:1, 81-112

Hattie, J. (2009) *Visible Learning*, Routledge

Hattie, J. (2012) *Visible Learning for Teachers*, Routledge

Hayes, JR. (2012) 'Modeling and remodeling writing', *Written Communication*, 29:3, 369-388

Holdsworth, S, Turner, M, and Scott-Young, CM. (2018) '...Not drowning, waving. Resilience and university: A student perspective', *Studies in Higher Education*, 43:11, 1837-1853

Kardas, M, and O'Brien, E. (2018) 'Easier seen than done: merely watching others perform can foster an illusion of skill acquisition', *Psychological Science*, 29:4, 521-536

Khattab, N. (2015) 'Students' aspirations, expectations and school achievement: what really matters?', *British Educational Research Journal*, 41:5, 731-748

Kluger, AN, and DeNisi, A. (1996) 'The effects of feedback interventions on performance: a historical review, a meta-analysis, and a preliminary feedback intervention theory', *Psychological Bulletin*, 119:2, 254-284

Mayer, RE, and Anderson, RB. (1991) 'Animations need narrations: an experimental test of a dual-coding hypothesis', *Journal of Educational Psychology*, 83:4, 484-490

Nestojko, JF, Bui, DC, Kornell, N, and Bjork, EL. (2014) 'Expecting to teach enhances learning and organization of knowledge in free recall of text passages', *Memory & Cognition*, 42, 1038-1048

Nicol, DJ, and Macfarlane-Dick, D. (2006) 'Formative assessment and self-regulated learning: a model and seven principles of good feedback practice', *Studies in Higher Education*, 31:2, 199-218

Nuthall, G. (2007) *The Hidden Lives of Learners*, NZCER Press

Rogers, LA, and Graham, S. (2008) 'A meta-analysis of single subject design writing intervention research', *Journal of Educational Psychology*, 100:4, 879-906

Rosenshine, B. (2012) 'Principles of instruction: research-based strategies that all teachers should know', *American Educator*, 36:1, 12-39

Saddler, B, and Graham, S. (2005) 'The effects of peer-assisted sentence-combining instruction on the writing performance of more and less skilled young writers', *Journal of Educational Psychology*, 97:1, 43-54

Sherrington, T. (2019) *Rosenshine's Principles in Action*, John Catt Educational

Troia, G. (2014) *Evidence-Based Practices for Writing Instruction* (CEEDAR document no. IC5), retrieved from University of Florida, Collaboration for Effective Educator, Development, Accountability, and Reform Center website: http://ceedar.education.ufl.edu/tools/innovation-configuration

Wiliam, D. (2006) 'Formative assessment: getting the focus right', *Educational Assessment*, 11:3, 283-289

Wiliam, D, and Thompson, M. (2007) 'Integrating assessment with learning: what will it take to make it work?' in Dwyer, CA (ed), *The Future of Assessment: shaping teaching and learning*, Erlbaum

Wiliam, D. (2013) 'Assessment: the bridge between teaching and learning', *Voices from the Middle*, 21:2, 15-20

Willingham, DT. (2006) 'How knowledge helps', *American Educator*, 30:1, 30-37